Play for Children with Special Needs

Play for Children with Special Needs

Including Children aged 3–8

Christine Macintyre

David Fulton Publishers
London

David Fulton Publishers Ltd
The Chiswick Centre, 414 Chiswick High Road, London W4 5TF
www.fultonpublishers.co.uk

First published in Great Britain in 2002 by David Fulton Publishers

David Fulton Publishers is a division of Granada Learning Limited, part of
Granada plc.

British Library Cataloguing in Publication Data
A catalogue record for this book is available from the British Library.

ISBN 1-85346-935-1

Typeset by FiSH Books, London
Printed and bound in Great Britain

Contents

Acknowledgements

My thanks go to all the children and adults – parents, teachers, nursery nurses and classroom assistants – who have been so generous in sharing their experiences and strategies which have helped children with special needs to play. All of these people have emphasised the value of play as the best mode of learning for their young children and they hope that others will have the confidence to let their children play too. Furthermore they emphasise that observation is best done while the children are at play, for then the children are relaxed and enjoying what they do. Observation can provide insights into what the children choose to do and what they avoid doing and this information can be vital in planning play episodes that will extend their learning. It can show the things the children are good at and those they need to practise. It can allow the adults to identify difficulties early so that the most appropriate kind of help is put in place. Surely then, no one could deny that play is a wonderful thing to do?

Thank you too to the delightful children who were photographed as they played. Some have special needs, others not, but they all demonstrated the skills which can be developed and the challenges which can be set in each aspect of learning – social, perceptual–motor, intellectual and emotional – and all of them happily through play.

My aim was to provide an introduction for adults wishing to know more about different special needs and to suggest 'play' ways through which the children might be helped. I hope I have.

Introduction

This book is all about letting children play, where necessary helping them to play and through that enhancing the learning of all young children as they play. It sets out to reassure everyone who looks after children that this is a good thing to do, because in play the children are free to make choices, to solve their own problems, to be responsible for themselves and their friends and to have fun. If anyone doubts that play is not the ideal way to learn, perhaps they would answer the question, 'What is it that children do not learn as they play?'

What do adults in school do then? Do they just stand back, I hear you ask? Surely if that is the case, they don't need all the professional education that they have? But of course the adults have a clear set of purposes in letting children play and these are arguably the most difficult to 'get right'. For the adults are observing each child very carefully in lots of different environments and building a profile of each child's capabilities and difficulties so that they can enhance each child's learning in the most appropriate way. What is involved in doing this? Well, the competences for observation cover each aspect of the child's development, i.e. social, emotional, perceptual–motor and intellectual, and observers have to understand the appropriate level of development in each, as well as appreciating how they interweave to influence the child that is the focus of study. This is not an easy thing to do. It takes time, patience and eyes that can see . . . for each child has an individual set of characteristics which determine how learning will be approached and how they will react to the suggestions that are made. These, plus understanding the child's interests, allow adults to structure play episodes which will stimulate the child to learn more and as they do, the adults will gauge how to intervene or make informed decisions about staying back, so that they do not encroach on the children's discoveries and take the fun of learning and succeeding away from them and keep it for themselves.

And of course, there are things the children must learn. They have to cope with 'rules' about respecting each other and the resources that are provided. Letting children play does not mean having a free for all where no one is heeded. These rules provide security and keep the children safe. They can still be learned through play.

And what of the children who find it difficult to play? Do the adults stand back then? If the children have specific difficulties that could hamper their play and their learning, the adults must certainly be aware of these and do their best to offset their effects. Very often the adults have to become the play partners for a time until the children learn to relate to some friends. But again this kind of intervention is based on assessing what the children can do and what they need help to do and developing their learning based on these observations.

Whenever the words 'special needs' are mentioned, the argument about inclusion usually follows. Should children with special needs be with all the others in mainstream education? The parents must make the choice. Their decision will to some extent consider their child's level of difficulty and the need for specialist teaching, as well as any special equipment and resources that their child requires. The question of auxiliary help in the classroom is important, although parents would wish to be reassured that the actual teaching is done by the teacher, for each child in the class has an equal right to teacher time. Practical concerns, such as how far the school is from the children's home, related to the mobility and independence the child has and whether family can help out in times of illness, are important influences on decisions too.

A more subtle worry may concern the parents of the other children, for they could resent the extra time which the children with special needs may require, and fear that their own children will be deprived in some way. The 'other' children are important too. Are they likely to be patient and welcoming, or will they latch on to the differences and exacerbate the difficulties of the children with special needs? And if they do, what policies has the school to deal with traumas and is there evidence that strategies emanating from these policies are in place? All of these are important factors in deciding where the children should go to school.

There is much evidence to show that children with special needs 'do better' in a mainstream setting, but parents, teachers and all the carers who support the policy of inclusion, must be able to articulate that there are benefits for all the other children too. What are these? Surely these young children must learn:

- that everyone is different – and so they learn to appreciate their own profile of competences and difficulties alongside those of the children with special needs;
- to understand the difficulties which the children with different special needs conditions have and through that learn patience and tolerance;
- that material things are less important than social skills such as sharing and waiting while others have a turn;
- that they themselves can act as a role model in helping others in all aspects of their learning;
- that they should look beyond the special need to see the child within as a person just as important as themselves.

Surely these lessons are critically important? And furthermore, without the special needs children in the class, they might not be learned at all.

Record keeping is an essential part of teaching all children; for the children with special educational needs even more so. This is because all the professional groups who are concerned to help will want to know the outcome of activities, or results of therapy, so that further development can be planned. Fortunately nowadays, there is much more communication between all those who are there to help the children – parents, therapists, teachers, nursery nurses, classroom assistants and special needs auxiliaries all have a very important and responsible role to play. They all contribute to the children's development. This book is written for all of them – to try to help in some small way, i.e. to ease the tremendously taxing job that they do. I hope it does.

Chapter 1 explains what play is, justifies it as the best learning medium for all children and suggests adaptations which could make it easier for children with special needs to play. Chapter 2 looks at the developmental changes that occur as children play so that observers may understand the changes, structure the play environment and make appropriate interventions should they be required. Chapter 3 gives a brief outline of some of the special needs conditions that have their own characteristics but urges adults to remember that there is rarely a 'typical' child, and that careful observation in the light of this understanding is the best way to take learning forward. Chapter 4 stresses the importance of communication among those who look after the children and tackles two issues which concern every adult who cares: how to keep the children's self-esteem high and how to tackle bullying. Finally Chapter 5 describes lots of activities for children that can promote learning in the best way of all, i.e. through having fun as they play.

CHAPTER 1

Play – what it is and its importance for children with special needs

Chapter 1 considers two questions, namely 'What is play?' and 'Why is play so critically important for children with special needs?'

What is play?

There are many people who have attempted to define play in a way which encapsulates all of its special qualities but although this would seem to be quite straightforward – for we have all played, haven't we? – this is not an easy thing to do. It has even been said that 'play is as elusive as the wind and can no more be caught by theory than wind can be caught in a paper bag!' (Reilly 1974). Frustration has often led to conclusions such as, 'Well...play is everything that is not work, is it not?' but assertions like this don't take understanding forward in any significant way. One definition does do this – one of the most helpful and thought-provoking definitions in my view and certainly one of the most enduring. It was penned by Susan Isaacs in 1933 when she wrote, 'Play is a child's life and the means by which he comes to understand the world around him.' This poetic description emphasised the importance of play in the child's development, but still the words need to be carefully analysed if we are to fully appreciate what she meant.

In the first part of the quotation, 'Play is a child's life...', she emphasises the pervasive nature of play, stressing that it makes up every part of the child's day. In so doing she makes us realise that young children do not differentiate between play and work in the way that adults do; she asserts that all the activities that children do should be called 'play'. What evidence led her to make this claim?

Her observations of very young children, even babies, at play showed that they were active young people who constantly set themselves problems and challenges, for example 'How can I make the music box on the side of the cot play?' or 'What kind of cries are going to bring Mum running?' And because these learning strategies were self-set, they were at the correct developmental level; with practice they were achievable. All of the children, without any adult intervention, were able to choose appropriate activities for themselves and found this pleasurable and satisfying. For when their problem was solved, when the music played or when Mum appeared, the children showed their delight by waving their arms and legs (i.e. through increased activity) and sometimes by gurgling or babbling (i.e. making the first language sounds) to convey their joy. Through this they were beginning to develop their communication skills. And so from the very earliest days, the children were learning through play. They chose what they wanted to do, they were able to repeat the activity to savour their success, or they could develop it, perhaps by being more precise in their reaching and grasping, or using more strength so that the music played for longer, or indeed they could decide to abandon that activity and go on to something else. What kind of learning goes on in activities like this? Let's analyse a different activity and find out.

Think of a toddler banging a drum. He quickly learns how to make a most satisfactory noise and for several days he really enjoys the activity, indeed he insists on having his drum! But suddenly the drum holds no more fascination for him and he moves on to try, possibly to demolish, something else. What has he learned? What kind of experiments will he have tried and, given that he has been fascinated by drumming, why should the drum suddenly be cast aside?

At first, beating the drum gives the child a sense of power. He is in charge, he can control what he does and if he bangs the drum hard enough Mum comes running so he influences her actions as well. This is very satisfying and because he smiles and coos Mum doesn't take the drum away, indeed she may praise him for having the coordination to play it in the first place. This is a very successful outcome to the problem, 'How do I play this drum and how do I get attention?' In the learning process he will have found the place to hit the drum where it makes most noise, although to begin with he will probably have experimented with hitting the side and the base as well as the skin and tried out both ends of the drumstick. In perfecting the hitting action he is learning about direction and rhythm and the amount of strength he needs to create different noise effects. He is learning how to hold the drumstick and how to let go – often the trickier move. But suddenly, and often to adults inexplicably, the activity is over and done with. He has had enough, the drum is valued no longer and another challenge takes its place.

Do you think that this would be the same for older children? Do they set themselves challenges for a time and then abandon them? Think of playground games. Suddenly skipping ropes or cards for collecting appear and just as suddenly they go. There doesn't seem to be an obvious reason for this. No one tells the children what to do and yet there seems to be a wave of agreement that makes the activity disappear.

Are there any theoretical explanations to tell us why this sequence of events takes place? Piaget (1969) offers one. He claims that children are born with enquiring minds and that it is this intrinsic motivation that keeps children playing and learning. They don't need adults to tell them what to do. If anyone doubts this, try taking a child for a walk. They won't walk sedately, they will run and skip and jump, or climb on walls, or play hopscotch as they go, for walking by itself doesn't hold nearly enough challenges. The children are experimenting with different skills that need more energy, balance, coordination and control than walking does. Interestingly, as they mature they don't do this any more. Perhaps as they go back to walking, other challenges, possibly intellectual ones such as what have I to buy?, take over instead or perhaps cultural influences have persuaded them that it is not the thing to do?

Throughout childhood, children practise a skill and the feedback they get from the result encourages them to continue. But when they become repeatedly successful in their own judgement, the skill holds no more challenge and they abandon it to try something else. Similarly, if they are consistently unsuccessful they give up trying. It seems that intermittent feedback is the result that keeps children longer on task – an important point for those planning teaching.

Another important feature of play activities is that the freedom children have to make their play choices gives them a sense of ownership and satisfaction, which in turn boosts their confidence. There is no sense of 'having to do something' or 'having to do it neatly' in a way which would conform to some externally imposed standard. This means that children at play have no fear of failure. And so, as they play they can experiment with objects and learn about their properties (e.g. hardness, softness, malleability, size in relation to other objects, taste and smell) in a childlike way. They can pretend that a yo-yo is a dog on a lead or that a brick is a lorry and no one will tell them that this is not the case or urge them to substitute a different toy. This means that the children can have fun. They can also use their imaginations and be engrossed in activities or in a dream world that adults may not understand. But they need time and space and freedom to do this.

There is another good thing about play which is destroyed when activities become work, for children can enjoy the process of playing without being concerned to make something recognisable, or in other words an end product. This means that the children can be in charge of their own learning; they can decide on the content, the pace and the resources they need; they can set themselves problems and decide whether or not to solve them. And as all of this happens in (usually) a secure environment where experimentation with new ideas is safe, the children can take risks, which enable them to learn new things. Think of a young boy clambering up the stairs. The success and the joy is in the climbing action – he's not going anywhere, just climbing for the sake of it! And it's just as well Mum's there because he hasn't worked out how to get down! He is enjoying the activity for its own sake and learning about coordination and balance as he goes. Surely this sounds an ideal way to spend the day?

From this explanation, we can elicit some criteria that describe play. These are that play:

- is enjoyable, because activities are freely chosen by the child – it is fun;
- can be abandoned without blame or fuss;

- has no preconceived outcome or end product so planning can happen as play goes on;
- gives pleasure and often counteracts stress;
- usually happens in a supervised environment, so children can take 'risks' and try out new moves – in this way they learn about keeping themselves safe;
- holds lots of potential for learning.

Doesn't this sound a good thing for children to do? And if you agree, shouldn't children with special needs be given even more time to play?

This brings us to the second question, 'Why is play critically important for children with special needs?'

Why is play critically important for children with special needs?

It goes without saying that all of the benefits already mentioned apply. Any change needs to be in time and support rather than restricting freedom in making choices. The adult needs to follow the children and find the most appropriate and often subtle way to extend learning possibilities rather than imposing other sorts of things for them to do. Perhaps adding a dumper truck to the sand tray will allow children who have been making roads to realise that there are mechanical ways to help and this could stimulate their interest in finding how they work. Perhaps children who don't see very well would enjoy brightly coloured ice cubes going into the warm water tray. If they have been pouring and learning about the properties of water (its volume, its weight, how pouring quickly and slowly gives different sound effects) and appear ready to go off somewhere else, seeing the bright colours may encourage them to stay a little longer and enjoy watching the ice cubes melt. They will also learn about the changing properties of water... and how they can assist the melting process by swirling the water around. And all of this can happen without a word from an adult. This allows the children to stay 'in charge' of the activity. The satisfaction and the success are theirs (Figure 1.1).

Despite all the benefits which have been set out, many people remain concerned that 'valuable learning time' will be lost if children with special needs are allowed lots of time to play. Perhaps observers have claimed that children 'aren't doing very much as they play' or that 'the children are doing the same thing over and over again' and they would prefer to involve them in a more formal teaching way. From their careful observations, they may wonder if the intrinsic motivation which Piaget (1969) claimed all children have, is present to the same extent in children with special needs. Hutt (1979) provides us with insights here. She explains that during play and learning, children engage in two kinds of activity. Although the formal names she gives these times are 'epistemic' and 'ludic' activity, simpler terms would be 'progress' and 'practice'. She explains that each type of play houses both of these elements. When the children learn something new, this is epistemic activity or

Figure 1.1 Children learning about the properties of water and how to control the flow

progress and when they repeat it with little or no change this is ludic activity or practice (see Appendix 1). Now the rate at which different children can absorb new things – so that the practice time required is shorter or longer – possibly marks the different rate of acquisition of skills for children with and without special needs or learning difficulties. Interestingly the same kinds of activities can fit into one column or the other depending on the level of proficiency of the player. Games with rules, such as a game of snakes and ladders, might be immediately seen as 'play as learning' but if one player was much more competent than the other, then the two players' skills really belong on different sides of the divide. This means that making decisions about the learning going on within play are more likely to be accurate if something of the player's experience and something of the playing context is known. Again this emphasises the falseness of making judgements based on little information. Similarly two children playing in the sand will have different time needs depending on their previous encounters with the medium, as well as the complexity of what they are attempting to do.

It takes a great deal of experience to know when to urge children to 'move on' and change their activity. Perhaps children with special needs just require a little longer to make choices and to solve problems (e.g. How does that shape go through that hole?) or to remember where the dressing up clothes are kept, or how to organise their resources ready to begin. And when they have decided what to try, i.e. to make up their own play activity, they may need longer to practise, to reinforce and internalise the learning that has occurred. Perhaps they need more time to appreciate what is going on around them, to plan what they would like to do or to consider ways in which they can interact successfully with other children or adults. Perhaps they don't have many ideas of their own and they are learning by watching what other children do. If more time is required – and after all there's lots of it – attempting to rush the children or suggesting alternative ways they might behave, only makes them stressed and confused. Before intervening at all, it is vitally important that observers try to understand these children's perspectives and through recognising them, appreciate their developing understanding, i.e. the learning that is going on ... for assuredly that is happening. Vygotsky (1978) is only one author who tries to reassure doubters when he claims that in play, 'A child is always above his average age ... in play it is as if a child is trying to jump above the level of his usual behaviour.' Can this be because there is no fear of failure, the children feel secure enough to try?

But of course, if children are bewildered by the play environment, they may need a more obvious guiding hand. Some children find it difficult to formulate ideas, to know what to do. They will need the kind of intervention which says 'Come on, let's try...' until the time that they have the confidence and competence to be more independent. In these circumstances the aim is that the shared activities should be mutually enjoyable. Observations should alert the adult to recognising the time when it is beneficial to gradually pull back. It can be very hard to do this, but keeping the three Ss in mind – *safety and stimulation without suffocation* – can prevent the adult being the main player with the child just lagging behind and learning nothing about decision making, problem solving or organising resources, competences they need as they mature.

Routines, memories and play

Linked with this idea of moving on to learn new things comes the realisation that some children want a tightly structured routine and become distressed by even minimal change. They want to have the same toys, the same stories, the same order of events during the day. Change appears to leave them vulnerable and unsure.

Why should routine be so important for some children? Perhaps it has to do with their short-term memories. The things which children do regularly become habitual – well known and able to be successfully achieved and so they give comfort and security. If children have poor short-term memories and can't recall what went on yesterday, they can't build on that experience without lots of reminders and prompting. If this is done publicly, then it can be a source of humiliation because the children realise that everyone else remembers while they don't. To prevent this arising, the children prefer things that they can remember, things that have become habitual or grooved. Then they are sure they can cope and so they are freed to anticipate what comes next or plan their next move. Very gradual change has to be planned for these children. Adults' observation will serve to note where the children spend most time and are most relaxed. Perhaps that activity could be retained until the children signal that they could tolerate some (small) change to it. Sudden changes that will stimulate and motivate lots of children can have the opposite effect on others, sometimes causing real distress and confusion, especially if the children are unable to explain what is wrong.

Many adults are fearful that children will become bored or stop learning if things stay too much the same. Perhaps they are reflecting on what they themselves experienced as learners? Gauging the pace of change for a group of children with very different abilities and needs is not easy. Observation and recording so that adults have a real picture, i.e. evidence of what really occurred and for exactly how long, makes for a useful group discussion and can be the source of getting extra advice from psychologists or linked professionals (see Appendix 4). It is ideal if one person can be given the role of 'observer only' for a time so that a range of observations in different environments can be taken unobtrusively. This is more useful than having a number of 'impressions' about how the children behaved on a 'vague' number of occasions, taken by adults trying to do all the things they have to do, because in such a busy setting, the adult's attention may have been distracted at the critical time when change was occurring. It would be important that the observer was rotated so that different observations were contrasted and compared. This would also help to reduce bias (i.e. any charge that observations taken by just one person might be inaccurate).

Structuring the play environment

Some critics of the child-centred way of promoting learning, point to what they see as lack of structure and describe it as a 'woolly' or *laissez-faire* way to teach. They have not understood that the play environment is as carefully structured as in any other learning mode, in fact possibly more so, as the content of learning corners (see Appendix 2), displays. Stories and other learning episodes are justified according to the children's interests, experiences and learning capacities rather than to some abstract notion of 'what children of five should be able to do'. These criteria are certainly not ignored in a child-centred framework as the norms of development are carefully considered in monitoring the children's progress. If they are not being achieved then steps are taken to find activities – still based on the children's interests and previous learning experiences – which would facilitate their achievement.

Example of promoting learning in a child-centred way

Alex came into nursery and announced that he would 'quite like to be blind because then he would get a guide dog'. This led to a small group discussion on what it would be like not to be able to see . . . and the children volunteered things that they would miss. Football matches and television were high on their list of priorities, until one little boy exclaimed that he would miss 'seeing my mummy's face', whereupon most of the other children suddenly became concerned to show they were caring people too. (That mum left the nursery with tears streaming down her face when she heard what Alex had said!)

This interaction led to a teaching input on 'the senses', which helped the children recognise how they perceived their world, thus contributing to their 'understanding of the world around them'. The children were all given a jelly baby (no vegetarians who couldn't have gelatin or children with allergies were present). They were to use their senses to investigate – a scientific experiment, the only 'rule' being that using the sense of taste came last! They felt the sweet (touch) and proclaimed it 'squidgy' and 'soft' and one child said 'bouncy'. These were good words to add to their vocabularies and because they came from the children themselves, they enjoyed repeating them and finding if feeling the jelly baby gave them that kind of sensation. Then the children were asked to describe their sweet, to discover what their visual sense told them. They volunteered colours and descriptive words such as 'plump', 'tiny'. Then one child said 'stooky' which prompted a discussion on what he meant. He explained that his choice of word was to show that the jelly baby's arms were 'stuck to its sides'. The children had fun walking around the room with their hands held into their sides and found how difficult balancing was. (This was a useful body awareness and movement lesson in miniature.) The staff could also look for movement learning difficulties such as identifying children who found it difficult to walk without swaying, i.e. children who needed the extra balance their arms usually gave. Then the children had to use their sense of smell. 'Tangy', 'sweet', 'icing sugary', were some descriptors which the children suggested, until the taste sense let them all enjoy their sweet. Chewing elicited that 'rubbery' was an apt description!

All of this came from one child's interest in dogs. The development that followed was enjoyed by everyone. The teachers claimed that everyone who wants to teach this way has to have the confidence that the children have the best ideas to take their own learning forward. All it needs is for teachers to listen and then think about how the children's ideas can be developed, remembering the kind of contribution that each child would be able to make. Added to that is the very real possibility that children will remember because of the fun they have had.

The discussion could well have followed a different route, perhaps learning more about dogs or the responsibility of keeping pets. As the staff followed the children's ideas, they were also keeping in mind the competences set out in curriculum guidance for the early years (Scottish Consultative Committee on the Curriculum 1999) and ensuring that they were covered.

In the second part of the quotation on p.1, Isaacs (1933) claims that through play the child 'comes to understand the world around him'. Like Vygotsky she is emphasising how much children learn as they play. But what sorts of understandings does she mean and what can be done to help children who need longer to understand and who need a greater amount of support and encouragement to make the shift from the practice to the progress mode? It is important to know, because the expectations of those who define the norms of behaviour and achievement are based on what most children are able to do at different ages. This information comes from studying children's development and allows identification of children with difficulties so that help can be quickly given.

How can we begin to understand children's development? Given the myriad of things children have to learn if they are to cope in a complex world, how can we know what the key competences are? Further, recognising the erratic nature of development, how can we know whether maturation and experience will alleviate any difficulties, or if intervention needs to be planned to help the children overcome them?

One important fact is that all children pass through the same stages of development. They learn to do the same kinds of things in the same order. Some go quickly, some more slowly, some more erratically than others with lots of stops and starts and certainly the final level of achievement is different, but there are things that every child will do. Recognising when these happen is the way to pinpoint individual development. But there are lots and lots of things and a list containing them all would soon become unmanageable. One strategy, which helps us to get to grips with the complexities of development, is to subdivide the topic into four aspects:

- social
- perceptual–motor
- intellectual
- emotional

and assign different competences under the appropriate heading (Figure 1.2). This lets us identify competences for assessment in each curriculum area – and implicitly highlights what needs to be taught if the children don't achieve these competences naturally as they play. (An explanation of specific difficulties comes in Chapter 3.)

These lists are formulated as summaries of those found in the *Curriculum Guidance for the Foundation Stage* (DfEE 2000) in England and the curriculum for children 3–5 document in Scotland (Scottish Consultative Committee on the Curriculum 1999) and the new early learning goals set out in the Framework of Nationally Accredited Qualification in Early Years Education (QCA 2001). The content is broadly the same, for example knowing right from wrong is subsumed under 'respecting self, other people and resources'. In my view, this arrangement shortens the lists and makes handling the competences more manageable. One set

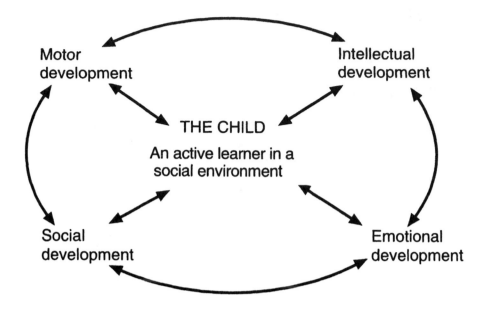

Figure 1.2 The different aspects of development

of original lists is in Appendix 3 for reference if this is required. The aspects of development organisation link closely to norms of development which are helpful in identifying difficulties in children with special needs. It also fits readily with the developmental stages of play outlined in Chapter 2.

The key competences and how they would be assessed

Social development

Social development is assessed in terms of the increasing competence children show in building relationships with adults and their peer group. This allows them to react appropriately in groups and in different social/cultural situations and very often is the basis for them making friends.

Social skills that would be assessed in the early years are:

- having the confidence to speak with adults and children outside the primary care group;
- interacting appropriately with adults and children;
- being willing to listen and respect another's point of view;
- being able to take turns;
- serving others, e.g. at snack;
- having a friend;

- looking out for someone less able;
- being willing to praise others;
- enjoying joining in.

Many parents and teachers identify the importance of social development, for children who are happy to interact in a group are likely to be confident enough to relax and learn from the others. Moreover, being accepted as part of a group or team gives confidence that spills over into other areas of learning. Vygotsky's (1978) idea of 'the zone of proximal development' and Bruner's (1966) concept of scaffolding both talk of how children's learning can be enhanced by others, even if they are only slightly more informed than they are themselves. Such findings led to the implementation of much group work, because in that social organisation, the children were supposed to learn more easily than if they tried to do so alone.

What difficulties might children with special needs have in being able to do these social activities?

Some children will have communication problems. One area of difficulty stemming from their inability to hold eye contact, i.e. to look at people as they speak, cuts down the opportunities for interaction, as 'eyes looking away' signal that the conversation is of no interest. This is off-putting for children who have initiated the interaction. They feel rebuffed, perhaps even intimidated by the unexpected response. If so, they are not likely to try again. Sadly this may be a 'successful' strategy for children with aspects of autism as they are trying to avoid communication; in fact adults with autism, reflecting on their childhood, tell how very difficult it was to try to hold gaze. Some children do not understand the mechanics or technique of dialogue and have to be taught the essence of how communicating takes place.

To help children converse, the first thing for adults to recognise is that conversations can be based on simple games which require turn taking, i.e. any game where 'I do' then 'you do'. Things like building a tower of bricks together (and then the child knocks it down), playing snap, or if the children have good fine motor skills, spilikins. Turn taking can come through singing nursery rhymes if the adult says the first part and lets the child come in with the punch line. Similarly with stories like 'The little red hen' where there is a great deal of repetition and the children can anticipate where they have to come in, with the famous line, 'then I'll do it myself!' Adults should reinforce turn taking as the game unfolds, saying for example 'my turn, your turn' because some children won't realise that this is the way conversations happen.

The next stage could be for the adults to choose a topic they know will motivate the children to respond and to try to develop a conversation based on that. Again they should emphasise the mechanics, 'I said...' and then 'you said', always encouraging the child by making positive comments, e.g. 'That was really interesting.' As this begins to be established the adult, sitting at the same level as the child, should try to hold gaze, even encouraging the child, 'Tell me and look at me, so that I can see what your eyes are saying...'.

Some children, but by no means all, who cannot interact appropriately with others, have come from homes where their role models shout and resort to hitting to vent their displeasure. They need time to relearn how to communicate and how to deal with upsets without resorting to aggression. This can take time and subtlety, because the child is dealing with conflicting messages in different environments. Some children quickly adapt, others take longer and some may be resentful if they suspect that their home ways are found to be unacceptable.

The strategy to help would seem to be to have these children imitate and so internalise acceptable ways. Providing a role model who demonstrates 'good behaviour' and who explains the reasons why this is a good way of doing things, can be very helpful. But some children cannot imitate without help – they have to be taught through special games based on 'follow me' or 'do as I do' rules. In this way an important competence, imitating, is being taught through play. Another strategy is to 'catch them being good' and give lots of praise – ignoring the bad behaviour when at all possible so that it doesn't have a 'reward', i.e. the attention that the child seeks.

Any intervention designed to modify the children's behaviour has to start from identifying the source of the children's difficulties and building small steps accompanied by lots of praise. It is important to keep to the same routine so that the children have a picture of what is going to occur. Especially for children with conflicting role models at home and at school, repetition gives security, for they learn what is acceptable in each place. This helps the children to be more confident in taking the next step forward.

Perceptual–motor development

Perceptual–motor development is assessed by observing if children learn to move efficiently and effectively in different environments, such as on large apparatus outside as well as being able to fasten buttons and zips. Both fine motor skills, which use the small muscle groups responsible for actions such as picking up objects, writing or drawing, and gross motor skills, such as running, jumping and climbing which depend on strength and length of limb as well as balance and coordination, require to be assessed. If difficulties are suspected, then the planning/organising of sequences of movement should be scrutinised as well as the more obvious assessment of the basic movement patterns themselves. This is because being able to move well depends on movement abilities, such as coordination and balance; perceptual abilities, such as sight, hearing and touching; and organisational skills, such as planning, ordering and sequencing. It is often very difficult to pinpoint the skill or skills which are causing the problem.

Skills that would be assessed in the early years are:

- being able to sit and stand still (this is harder than walking);
- the basic movement patterns, e.g. walking, running, skipping and hopping;
- fine movements, e.g. writing, threading, pouring and cutting;
- daily coping skills, e.g. getting dressed, wiping at the toilet;
- handling small apparatus, e.g. a bat and ball, the computer mouse;
- crawling;
- gaining control in carrying out all kinds of movements.

It is worth noting that if children have a learning difficulty, it can often be spotted first in poor movement coordination and in delay in reaching their motor milestones (Table 1.1). This early diagnosis allows the children to have the earliest possible help.

What difficulties might children with special needs have in being able to do these movement activities?

One of the telling assessments concerns the assessment of crawling, one of the basic movement patterns. This is because many children who don't crawl, just can't crawl. Their parents may be mistaken in thinking that they have jumped a developmental stage when indeed they do not have the coordination or the sequencing ability to carry out the action. I mention this particularly because although many 'non-crawlers' have no other difficulties, children with dyspraxia and/or dyslexia and other less specific learning difficulties are often found to be among this group. And so, if young children are showing movement difficulties – and it is estimated that 8–10 per cent of them do – it is a good idea to have a game involving crawling. Crawling through tunnels, through legs and even crawling up stairs with an adult behind are fun ways to try (Figure 1.3). If a child can't crawl, then immediate help is required, because the balance skills learned in crawling are essential to stability both in movement and in stillness. At the same time, sequencing appears to help reading and ordering events in activities like storytelling.

Many young children are clumsy. They bump and barge and seem to have permanently skinned knees. Some children will outgrow these difficulties as maturation and practice combine to help their performance. Others need to be helped to slow down and practise their basic patterns, firstly with no apparatus then with increasingly complex arrangements. For example they should learn to throw and catch a ball before they try to coordinate a bat and ball, or learn to kick a stationary ball before they try to run and kick. Lots of other children have perceptual–motor difficulties or dyspraxia, which means that they need programmes of activities that are carefully planned to develop their motor skills. These will be based on helping the movement abilities, such as balance, coordination, timing and pacing (rhythm), the perceptual abilities, such as kinesthetic awareness, and their sensory integration, can be helped through multisensory teaching.

Table 1.1 Early motor milestones

Age 6–8 months	– should be able to reach and grasp, but still will have difficulty 'letting go' – should be 'nearly sitting' unsupported for a short time – may be rolling over sideways
Age 9–12 months	– pulling up on furniture, attempting to stand with support – will be moving around – hopefully crawling
Age 1 year – 18 months	– walking and crawling intermittently – lots of bumping down. Some will scribble using a finger thumb pencil grip but often a clutched grip is used. No hand dominance at this stage.
Age 2 years	– immature running pattern evident now – may be little control in stopping Climbs stairs in a step feet together pattern. Can unscrew lids, thread beads and chat in longer phrases. Understands what is being said. Will rebel if displeased! Shows clear hand preference although some jobs can still be done with either hand.
Age 3 years	– confident running now. Jumping to have two feet off the ground still difficult. Combines movements, e.g. running to kick a ball – not always successfully. Attempts stairs with the mature fluent pattern. Catches a large soft ball.
Age 4 years	– pedals a trike now. Can run and jump to land on two feet. Can pour juice from a jug and wipe dishes. Can hammer nails and do jigsaws. Has a large vocabulary. Still concerned with 'own' events rather than appreciating other people's but developing altruism and empathy especially if role models are at hand.
Age 5 years	– can skip and follow a clapping rhythm now. Enjoys stories and rhymes. Likes to look after others and take responsibility. Likes to help organise and can tidy up. All the basic motor patterns should be achieved now.

NB the 'normal' age span for the development of the basic movement patterns is wide, but children markedly different from their peers should be checked out to see if extra help is required.

Children who don't crawl may not have the sequencing and coordination to allow them to do so. Instead of allowing them to miss this stage, crawling games and analysing the crawl pattern for the children can be helpful in giving the kind of balancing and reaching experience which they otherwise would have missed.

Helping children to move well is vitally important, as being unable to do things which are important to children, such as ride a bike, tie their laces or unscrew the lid of their juice beaker, spills over into all other areas of development. Moreover, movement skills are public and children can be cruel and those who are inept can be devastated by not being able to achieve things other children can do at the correct

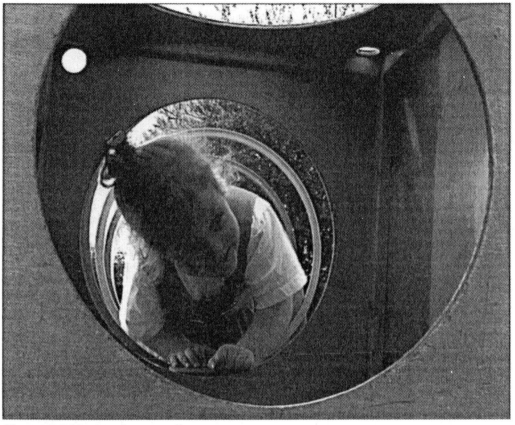

Figure 1.3 Having fun crawling

time, especially if these others point it out. They often conclude that they are no use, not just in the perceptual–motor domain, but no use at all – and as the early years' curriculum has a large practical component (Table 1.2), poor movement skills can impinge across the board giving a false picture of the children's ability. Very often poor muscle tone is at the root of the more severe difficulties and special strengthening programmes or physiotherapy is the best way to help.

When children have difficulties, the temptation is to do things for them, often just to save time. Some children resent this while others are happy for it to happen. However, a better strategy is to analyse each task and allow them to complete just one part – even carrying their bag out to the car or the bus gives them practice in lifting and lowering and helps them learn to balance carrying a weight, so there is lots of movement learning, even if the children can't fasten the bag itself. With activities like throwing and catching, having a larger, softer ball sympathetically thrown, can ease the time pressure for the children while still letting them feel they have participated in the game.

Table 1.2 Important practical skills within the early years' curriculum

Gross motor skills	Fine motor skills	Coping skills
Sitting still	Writing	Coats off and on
Standing still	Drawing	Coping at the toilet
Walking	Painting	Putting on a pinny
Running	Cutting	Sitting at snack
Crawling	Pouring	Running and stopping
Climbing	Spreading (at snack time)	without barging
Jumping	Modelling (in the sand)	Judging distances, e.g.
Throwing	Dressing up	how long to draw a line;
Catching	Gluing	how far to throw a ball
Kicking	Activities at the midline	Being able to wait for a turn
Turning corners	of the body, e.g.	Moving with control
Running: changing	winding a yo-yo	Using cups, plates, etc.
direction	Jigsaws and puzzles	Remembering where
		everything is

Intellectual development

In the early years, intellectual development may be assessed 'narrowly' by observing how children grasp early learning tasks, such as recognising their written names, whether they know their colours and can count, perhaps up to 20, in Class 1. But in a wider sense, intellectual development is evident in the children's use of resources. For example, how do they play in the house corner, can they set a table or understand what kinds of actions are appropriate in the hospital corner? When they visit the shop, do they understand the sequence of events implicit in buying and paying? Can they name the goods that they have bought? Do they know what they are for? Do they recognise some of the fruits, such as grapefruit and lemons, and if not, can they retain this information after they have been told? Do they have the language to explain? Even in the nursery, pre-reading skills (e.g. recognising their name on 'tickets' for snack or on their coat pegs, or explaining what they see in a picture) and basic arithmetic (e.g. matching shapes or correctly counting out three apples to sell in the shop corner) would be assessed along with problem solving (e.g. how they might construct a bus out of large wooden bricks). These would be in addition to more obvious assessments like how the children respond to stories (e.g. suggesting what might come next) or contribute orally in discussions (e.g. telling their own news or linking what has been said to their own experiences).

Intellectual skills that might be assessed in the early years are:

- knowledge and understanding of their world and to a lesser extent the world of other cultures;
- language (vocabulary, articulation and meaning, i.e. understanding words in context);

- communication skills (e.g. initiating and responding to interactions using appropriate tone and intonation);
- problem-solving abilities (e.g. selecting appropriate materials to complete a task);
- recognition of small numbers (e.g. that only four people are allowed on the climbing frame at once);
- basic mathematical competence (understanding what numbers mean; conceptual understanding of bigger, smaller, nearer, further away);
- ability to listen to a story and recount some of the detail;
- ability to concentrate for a reasonable length of time.

What difficulties might children with special needs have in being able to do these intellectual things?

Some children have a poor short-term memory and they become frustrated by not being able to remember and so not being able to do things they managed the day before. They need lots of calm repetition, to be asked to repeat things back and plenty of praise along with strategies to help them remember. Such strategies could include laminated sheets which perhaps depict the letter learned that day, to take home, or picture boards reminding them of the activities for the day.

Five-year-old children have made the timetable shown in Figure 1.4 to remind them of what happens next in the day. For the older children, see-through pencil cases can contain timetables and reminders of any unusual happenings, for example 'remember to go home with Jill today'. These are very useful, giving children the opportunity to be independent. Adults have to understand that poor auditory sequential memory is not laziness or inattention, although children with this difficulty can be guilty of these traits too.

Some children have an extensive vocabulary but don't appear to understand the meaning of some of the words they say. This lack of understanding can be overlooked because of the fluency of the child's language, or because the grown-up words they use mask the difficulty which then becomes apparent in other activities, such as if events in a story have to be remembered, or if the child has to think of descriptive words which are suitable for a picture or they are asked to explain the meaning of the word they have used.

Concentration skills help the children stay on task, so that they learn well. If some find this difficult the teacher has to conceptualise short activities that cover the key skills (see Chapter 5), hoping that they will be internalised before the concentration goes. Sometimes rewards – if they are meaningful to the child – can help a child to complete a task and then the praise can engender further motivation, but many children amaze adults by the length and quality of concentration they show if they are intrigued by what they are trying to do (Figure 1.5).

Figure 1.4 Six-year-olds make their timetable to give a visual aide-memoire

And so helping the children who have difficulties involves the same careful preparation and planning episodes of good teaching, where the adults:

- observe and analyse the children's interests;
- know their responses in different environments;
- gauge how much new learning is likely to be absorbed;
- recognise the way the children learn most easily;
- prepare materials which satisfy these criteria;
- ensure that the resources are the most suitable and that they reinforce the key elements of the learning episodes;
- make informed, justifiable decisions about intervention or non-intervention;
- make sure that the children are properly settled so that they can learn with minimum distractions.

As with all learning difficulties, it is essential to distinguish between a delay and a disorder, for while the child may catch up once a delay has been overtaken, a specific disorder needs professional diagnosis and help (see Chapter 3).

Figure 1.5 Child concentrating hard, cutting with left-handed scissors

Emotional development

Emotional development is assessed by studying how children's feelings and perceptions affect their behaviour and learning. This is perhaps the hardest to assess because 'improvements', such as an increase in confidence, are most apparent when the children become able to do other things. In addition, the observers may require to monitor non-verbal behaviour – for example holding eye contact, not encroaching on another person's personal space, how children interpret facial expressions during interactions – and this can be extremely difficult. Criteria such as 'willingness to get involved' are quite woolly yet they are very important because this could be a measure of raised self-esteem. The development of imagination and creativity comes under this heading too, as does aesthetic appreciation. These are all difficult to assess yet if they are ignored then no one can claim that they have looked at the whole child. Children with special needs may have a particular strength in this area and may show their developing competence through some art work or drama when they may not have the vocabulary or the confidence to express their stories or their feelings orally.

Emotional skills that would be assessed in the early years are:

- altruism – do the children care for others and understand their hurt?
- respecting self, other people and resources;
- the way in which feelings and emotions are expressed;
- the way the children cope, i.e. with resilience or vulnerability;
- confidence in starting out to do something new;
- willingness to share anxieties;
- willingness to be approached by (approved) strangers;
- willingness to offer suggestions/opinions;
- willingness to accept praise.

The personality traits of resilience or vulnerability are interesting and relevant here because they influence the children's perceptions of what is going on around them, as well as how they cope with any incident in the day. In the same situation, resilient children can shrug off real or imagined hurts while more vulnerable ones are devastated and need time and support to recover their equilibrium. This can affect the way children view learning opportunities too. The resilient ones will tend to see 'the good things' and so be ready to participate, while the vulnerable ones will anticipate all the difficulties, get them out of proportion, dispute any reassurances and often refuse to take part at all.

Example

Liam came into the hall and found Harry sitting in 'his' space on the floor – right in the centre of the coloured circle drawn on the floor. Liam complained bitterly and Harry retorted, 'I was here first!' Impasse! Luckily when Harry saw how upset Liam was – he was beginning to tremble and cry – Harry shrugged and ran off, unfortunately calling out 'cry baby' as he went.

The teacher was relieved to have avoided any confrontation, but was left wondering whether that outcome was the best resolution. What do you think she should have done? Would you agree or could you suggest another way? Should she intervene with Liam and Harry or leave well alone and hope that this was a one-off incident? It would be unrealistic for those who don't know the children to be sure, but episodes like this, even hypothetical possibilities, do make good discussion points.

Quite a common emotional difficulty becomes apparent when children fail to appreciate someone else's perspective, i.e. that others may have viewpoints that are different to their own. This can cause confusion and breakdown in conversations with children finding it difficult to play together.

Some children and adults fail to appreciate the subtle nuances that give meaning to language, not appreciating that the words themselves only hold a small part of the meaning. They can then lose the track of conversations because the actions don't relate to the words that they hear. Staff may use expressive sarcasm legitimately if it is to stimulate the children to respond and doesn't have any personal vibes, for example 'We all enjoyed the Giant's dinner of slugs and seaweed, didn't we?' However, when this happens, the children who don't understand the intonation which shows that this comment is not true, are left wondering why the accompanying gestures signal horror or even being sick! Similarly some children may not realise when role play within a game stops and the children revert to being themselves again. Children rarely put out markers to signal the end of an episode; they don't say, 'That's the end,' and their changes in behaviour may be so subtle that they bypass children who are not particularly perceptive.

Occasions like these mean that it can be hard for children with difficulties in interpreting non-verbal behaviour, or who use literal interpretations of meanings from interactions, to make and retain friends. They tend to be isolated or resort to aggression or withdraw from activities because they do not understand what is going on. Explanations and repetitions of similar activities and lots of stories with pauses to ask, 'How do you think (the character feels)?' or 'Why did . . . say . . . ' or sharing the real or imagined experiences of a favourite toy are good strategies to help.

Once the children come to realise that their friends have different experiences to themselves and so have different responses and evaluations, the next development could be to discuss, 'Well, what shall we do?' This would allow the children to discuss various responses while they were in a sheltered setting and build on the realisation that different ways were acceptable because the adult could then develop the conversation by anticipating the consequences of each suggestion that had been made.

Interactions

Of course the four aspects of development interact and progression, or indeed regression, in one aspect impinges on all of the others. The arrows in Figure 1.2 show how this happens. This is also why observation should encompass more than one activity or aspect of daily living on several occasions and in different environments. Only in this way can observations be accurate and pinpoint any underlying difficulty. The following examples demonstrate the interactions between the four aspects of development.

Example 1

Think of Jamie who had been toilet trained successfully at home, but who comes to nursery and has regular accidents. The first thought could be that this could be down to stress and that being in a new environment has caused the child to regress to an earlier stage of emotional/physical development. Whether this regression will have lasting impact or just be a blip in progress depends on the length of time the difficulty lasts, the reactions of adults at school and at home and how Jamie's personality enables him to cope with this undoubtedly distressing affair. It is not difficult to imagine the impact on his self-esteem, especially if other children notice and comment. If the difficulty persists, he may not be able to play away from home with friends until the problem is overcome. This could affect his social development.

However it could be that Jamie has forgotten where the toilets are (intellectual development) or indeed that something has alarmed him so that 'going' is avoided altogether. And of course he may lack the bladder control to hold on – lots of children with poor muscle tone in this region have accidents. This would show poor motor development. It may be a bladder infection, which needs antibiotics, but if children like Jamie can't or won't explain, the problem may take much longer to be resolved. Of course, one-off blips occur too especially on cold days or after lots of juice!

Example 2

One little girl came home from school wearing different pants. Investigating why, her mum was horrified to discover that 'My school doesn't have any toilets!' It transpired that because the child arrived late, she had missed the 'familiarisation walk' and because she was a quiet child, she had not followed any other child out of the main room to investigate. She was too small to rationalise that there had to be toilets and too timid to ask. The staff, noticing the puddle, had sorted this out, but not soon enough to avoid an accident.

Another group of children set themselves a competition to see 'who didn't go all day'. The staff wondered what they would think up next!

Example 3

Children who are newly able to swim have taken a huge stride forward in their perceptual–motor development and as a result other aspects of their development show gains too. Now that they are able to swim, they can interact with friends (a social gain); they have learned the names of different strokes and when they are best used (an intellectual gain); they can meet the technical demands of the stroke (a perceptual–motor gain) and possibly best of all, they become more confident in their own ability to learn a new skill (an emotional gain) which has a positive impact on their self-esteem. They are also likely to be praised and they may get a reward to mark their achievement. What happy children they are likely to be!

This is why Figure 1.2 has arrows linking the different subdivisions of development. They are to remind those who observe children, assess their progress and plan learning activities on that basis, that progress in one area is likely to benefit other areas as well. In a similar vein, new or unhappy experiences can cause children to regress to an earlier stage of development. If everyone recognises that this is quite a common state of affairs and that it is likely to be temporary, then the regression, although important, can be kept in proportion.

This interplay, however, means that sometimes it is difficult to know where to place different assessments. If a child is able to get dressed in an acceptable amount of time now (where previously that was really difficult), what kind of progress is that? Is it intellectual (the child can now understand the order of putting clothes on and gauge the time to be spent on each action)? Is it perceptual–motor (the child has now developed the coordination to be able to do up buttons and tie laces)? Is it emotional (the child has gained confidence from not being constantly chivvied, 'Come on, you're last again!')? In my view, considering progress across the spectrum and recording the changes is more important than worrying about having the assessments in the 'correct' place. In fact, different viewpoints of where they 'should' be placed, can form the basis of rich discussions about the children's progress.

It is also important to remember that each child is an individual and that no two conform to the same pattern. This makes caring for them properly and teaching them well a huge challenge and responsibility. The Scottish Consultative Committee on the Curriculum (1999) gives us a reminder. It says,

> Each child is a unique individual. Each brings a different life story to the early years' setting. Growing up as a member of a family and community with unique ways of understanding the world creates an individual pattern and pace of development.

So staff, with responsibility for 30 or so children, have a mammoth task in getting to understand each child as an individual, with different abilities, different likes and dislikes and different ways of coping with the highs and lows of the day.

CHAPTER 2

Stages in the development of play and difficulties for children with special needs

As children grow and mature in all aspects of their development, the type of play they choose to engage in changes too. This is in part due to their developing strength and length of limb (physical development), to their increasing perceptual acuity (vision, hearing, kinesthetic awareness) and to their increased experience and familiarity with their environment. Think of how the possibilities of exploring and discovering new things increase once children can crawl. The important thing is to realise that as the children move from one stage to the next (although it could be misleading to think of stages as abrupt changes because the behaviours of two stages mingle and mix for a time) the things the children play at are more demanding physically, intellectually, socially and emotionally. No one tells them to make the change or what the change entails, yet all children go through the same process just as they did with the stages of development. And in the same way, the pace of change varies and the final achievement is different, because only some children will successfully cope with the most challenging type of play, complex games with rules. Understanding the stages in play and their links to specific ages, provides a means of assessing development through play. A few children however, will have unusual pathways, such as the children who can play chess expertly yet find it very difficult to engage in role play at a basic level.

The stages in the development of play are:

- sensori-motor play 0–2 years;
- constructive play 2 years plus;
- pretend play 3–7 years;
- sociodramatic play 4 years plus;
- games with rules 7 years plus.

As these stages are described, the text will consider how children with special needs may have difficulties in progressing and suggest ways to help. But before that, a summary of some of the particular difficulties that make playing hard might be helpful.

Difficulties that make playing hard

Social difficulties

These include:

- being too timid to join in;
- being aggressive, and spoiling things;
- being reluctant to share;
- being unwilling to take turns;
- avoiding communication;
- inability to give and read non-verbal signals.

Perceptual–motor difficulties

These include:

- poor body awarenesss;
- clumsiness (poor coordination and balance);
- difficulty working at and crossing the midline of the body;
- poor fine motor control, e.g. in handling equipment/resources;
- hurting others through bumping and barging;
- hyperactivity or the inability to stand or sit still;
- difficulty in planning and organising self and the play resources.

Intellectual difficulties

These include:

- not knowing what to do;
- not being able to make suggestions to take the game forward;
- poor short-term memory, not remembering what went on before;
- poor verbal skills, e.g. limited vocabulary, remembering what was said;
- being unable to follow the 'rules' of the game.

Emotional difficulties

These include:

- being unable to understand pretending and/or imitating;
- little confidence;
- poor concentration, little tenacity;
- compulsive repetitive behaviour;
- low toleration of being touched;
- poor altruism or willingness to help others.

These lists of difficulties, just like the competences children are to develop, could become very long and those who are there to help the children could well feel overwhelmed by having to identify them all. One thing to remember is that some children will cope very well across the board, while others have a 'global developmental delay', which means that they will function across all aspects of development at a level of competence expected of a younger child. And there will be children who 'fit' every shade between. In assessing children who appear to be 'slow' in one, or more than one, aspect of development, completing a developmental record such as a checklist (see Appendix 4) can give an indication of how much delay there is. Some children will have only one or two minor difficulties and some will have several, more severely. Some will have a diagnosis of a specific condition, some not, but of course the important thing is assessing and helping the children's competence and through that fostering their confidence. It is more positive to understand specific learning difficulties and global developmental delay and use that information to establish a framework for reference, rather than using it to make prognoses about the child's learning potential, because all children can surprise and the effect of motivation should never be underestimated. Any difficulties need to be seen alongside the strengths that the children have (Chazan *et al.* 1987). It goes without saying that recognised tests have to be carried out by psychologists or paediatricians if a specific disorder is suspected.

Let's look now at the stages of play in more detail.

Sensori-motor play (sometimes called manipulation of objects)

This name indicates that children are taking information from the environment through their senses (perception); that they are using this information to guide their movements and that these movements in turn enable them to use more sensory information and practise more sophisticated movements.

Think of babies of six months or so who put everything they find in their mouths. They do this because this most sensitive area conveys sensory information to the cerebral cortex of the brain quickly. They are investigating the object that they hold and are learning about its properties, for example its hardness or softness; its shape; whether it changes shape in response to being sucked; what it tastes like; what kind of smell it has and whether it sticks to their hands or can be easily thrown away; whether it is heavy or light and can be passed from one hand to the other; what sound it makes when it is shaken or dropped and what kind of reaction sucking it brings from the adults around. There is such a lot of learning in this activity which all babies do.

But even before they can do these things the children have to get hold of the object in the first place. What does that involve? Think of a baby, sitting, wanting to grasp one of the toys just out of reach for example on a mobile. The key actions will be reaching and grasping.

In reaching, the decisions that have to be made are:

- which hand will I use? This develops a sense of hand dominance. A successful result will give positive feedback and encourage the same hand to be used again.
- direction – do I stretch out forwards, sideways, diagonally, even backwards? This helps spatial awareness and directionality.
- distance – how far away is it and do I need to adjust my position to get there? This helps both spatial and kinesthetic awareness.
- timing – when do I stretch out and how fast do I need to move? This helps directionality and pacing.
- balance – do I need to make any compensatory movements so that I won't fall over? This helps learning about stability.
- coping at the midline – how do I cope if the stretch should involve crossing the midline of my body? This helps hand dominance and coordination.

In grasping and releasing (i.e. opening and closing the hand) the decisions that have to be made are:

- timing – when should I open and close my fingers and when should I let go (the harder part of the action)?
- strength – how tightly do I need to grasp? What happens if I hold too tightly or not tightly enough?
- texture – how does the mobile feel? (This develops tactile sensitivity, but some children cannot tolerate some textures and this may cause them to avoid the activity.)
- reaction time – what happens when I let go? Can I avoid a swinging toy?

In all of this exploratory play, the children are learning how to handle objects with increasing dexterity and how objects react when they do things to them. One further very important aspect of learning in the perceptual–motor domain is that the babies are learning about their body boundary, where they end and the outside world begins. This is critical for later learning which involves handling objects, such as writing with a pencil, placing a cup on a table or hitting a ball with a bat. It is a central component of dexterity or adroitness, which also needs the appropriate kind of coordination.

All of these decision-making activities means that play can be hard work, requiring as it does lots of concentration, even resilience and determination to try again if the baby makes the wrong timing decision and the swinging object comes back to smack! And as they practise, the children are developing 'practical intelligence', i.e. a repertoire of skills which for most children will form the basis of a repertoire of many others (see the section on dyspraxia in Chapter 3).

But what about the children who can't reach out and grasp – what would seem, until the analysis, to be a relatively simple movement task? What sorts of things are holding them back?

Firstly, poor muscle tone may be the cause. This would be shown in lack of strength to grasp, which would hamper all aspects of the movement. Secondly not having the postural control, the balance to make the adjustment, may be another problem. Perhaps providing support at the child's back would take away this difficulty while having a soft ball that did not rebound in an alarming way would remove any sense of danger and encourage perseverance. If the object was still, rather than moving on a mobile, this would reduce the timing judgements and the children could more easily use vision to see when to open and close their hands.

How can little hands be strengthened? Squeezing a sponge with one or both hands is strengthening and a wet sponge in the bath provides plenty of fun and a most satisfactory result. Any play in water offers some resistance which strengthens, the best of all being swimming activities where all the limbs can move against the resistance of the water while the body weight is supported by it. Lots of finger games, such as 'Round and round the garden', allow babies to concentrate on their hands; slightly older ones enjoy 'Incy-wincy spider' and other rhymes. Strictly speaking, these kinds of activities help mobility rather than strengthening, which requires some resistance to make the muscles work hard, but they are useful in promoting body awareness as well as concentration. Luckily they are hugely enjoyable too.

What if a child has difficulty seeing and/or tracking the object?

If children are visually impaired, bright colours can help. Another useful ploy is having something that makes a noise, such as a soft pompom with a bell inside so that the children can use hearing, to help them place the object in space. They should be allowed to go as near the object as necessary to use what vision they have. Children who have poor vision may have related difficulties with balance, as visual cues that help stability are reduced. They also have fewer opportunities to learn through observation as the role model disappears more quickly – and in the nursery or classroom they may require extended explanations like 'Come and sit near the red table', rather than signals such as beckoning, as non-verbal communication may be missed.

Tracking is another difficulty. Some children may see the object in front of them but lose it when it goes out to the side. They may need to be helped to turn their heads to see, because some will believe that the object is no longer there if it has gone from their frontal visual plane. Gentle turning support, saying 'Look there', can help children to realise that objects are still present. This tracking skill needs to be developed so that later difficulties with for example copying from the blackboard or following the path of a ball, can be avoided.

If children are helped to turn their heads to the side, or indeed when they do this themselves, it is a good idea to see if there is any movement of the arm stretching out to the side. This could indicate the retention of the asymmetric tonic neck reflex that causes one action to influence the other. Specialists at the Institute for

Neuro-physiological Psychology in Chester make this kind of investigation the focus of their identifying children's difficulties. Peter and Sally Blythe, the Directors, provide a series of exercises to wash out primitive reflexes like this so that the postural reflexes can take their place. These allow more sophisticated movements to happen. Details can be found in Sally's book *A Teacher's Window into the Child's Mind* (Goddard 1996).

Some children find crossing the midline of the body very difficult and will use avoiding strategies to evade it. Observers will notice that these children don't pass objects from hand to hand but drop and retrieve them with the other hand instead. It is important to assist children to do this by gently bringing their two hands together at the midline and showing them how to grasp and how passing from one hand to the other is negotiated. This will help them develop a sense of hand dominance, which is helpful in avoiding confusion when it comes to writing, drawing, threading and cutting and many other activities of daily living.

Working at the midline of the body happens all of the time, although most people don't realise this or analyse it when it does. Such activities include tying laces, holding a jar to unscrew the lid, doing up zips, using a knife and fork, winding up a yo-yo, spreading toast and many more. Can you see the wide range of difficulties facing the children who cannot do these things? Children with motor learning difficulties (dyspraxia or developmental coordination disorder) feature in this group although clumsiness appears as a key identifying factor in a number of other conditions such as Asperger's syndrome, dyslexia and attention deficit hyperactivity disorder (ADHD) (see Chapter 3). Sometimes supporting the child at the back can help as this reduces the balance demands so the child feels secure and can concentrate on the task at hand.

A hearing difficulty may well impinge on children's ability to play, the most obvious reason being that the children are less aware of what is happening around them and may miss some verbal and non-verbal cues. This means that their reactions may be delayed and they are left behind. A more subtle disadvantage for the children is the fact that not hearing clearly may mean that they are startled, perhaps by someone approaching from behind, and their 'fright and flight' response causes them to withdraw from the activity. Although they may join in again quite soon, they may have lost confidence and need a lot of reassurance before cooperating fully again. They may then appear to be holding a little in reserve, a most understandable safety mechanism, but one that hampers full-hearted participation.

And of course, 'not knowing what to do' or not being able to plan how to do it is quite different from not having the movement ability to carry it out. This needs careful observation and possibly questioning if it is not to be confused by other difficulties. Trying to help may involve lots of suggestions so that the children can choose the best way for them.

The frustrating thing for some children with special needs is that they don't have the same ability to transfer their learning as other children do. Ayres (1972) explains that some children fail to habituate, i.e. to recall elements of previous learning and use them again. Instead they have to carry out every movement as if it was a first time try. Remember the stress of learning to drive? If this was to go on all day, can you wonder that 'these children have a very tiring day' (Chesson *et al.* 1990).

It should be noted that some of these difficulties can affect all different kinds of play while some are more specific to one developmental stage. This doesn't necessarily mean that the children have matured out of the difficulty – although they may have done so. It means that each type of play has its own set of demands, and so calls on a different range of competences.

Constructive play

Although some children engage in constructive play before they are mobile in the sense of being able to crawl or walk, generally this type of play is assigned to the children of 18 months or so because that's when they start to make things. For example they enjoy building in the most elementary sense such as piling bricks up and knocking them down again. Now they can use a pincer grip which eases grasping and letting go. From six months or so children will anticipate turn taking in a game such as peek-a-boo, but at this slightly later stage they will initiate a game rather than just respond to someone else's idea. Beyond 18 months the children become interested in problem solving, in discovering how to work the jack-in-the-box, in simple jigsaws and puzzles – hence the name 'construction'. Perhaps some parents would prefer 'destruction' as they see their cupboards being emptied but this could also be seen as problem solving – discovering what is stored in a cupboard – although the children rarely complete the solution by putting it back. At the two-year-old stage, toys are beginning to be used for their real purpose, i.e. a car is a car.

What about children with learning difficulties?

It may be at this stage that parents come to realise that 'something is amiss' because their children are not interested in construction toys. Perhaps they don't manage to hold the pattern of the jigsaw in their head as they manipulate the pieces; or they don't recognise how the pieces are supposed to fit together; or they lack the dexterity to complete the puzzle. Indeed they may lack the motivation or concentration to attempt this kind of activity at all. At this stage too, difficulties with coordination become more apparent as the children attempt to combine actions as they manipulate equipment. Frustration can lead to tantrums – hence the 'terrible twos'.

In construction activities, working at the midline of the body is especially important and this can cause real problems for children with midline difficulties.

Doing one action with one hand and something else with the other can demand too high a level of coordination, so tasks like holding a brick steady with one hand while balancing another on the top don't hold much chance of success.

While constructive play needs motor skills (Figures 2.1 and 2.2), it can be sympathetically and meaningfully extended to promote intellectual development too, for example asking 'How do builders make holes for windows and doors in real houses?' or making a statement 'I would like to live in a house like this.' This kind of interaction is more likely to encourage the children to carry on the conversation.

By this age, attempts should be made to encourage crawling in children who haven't volunteered to do so, because of the balancing and sequencing of actions which goes on while the children are in a safe prone position, and because of the possible links between crawling and competence in reading and writing. Toddlers with poor muscle tone in their legs are not likely to be walking by this age. How can they be helped? There is always a heated controversy about whether to wait for maturation to provide the necessary strength, coordination and balance or whether to attempt to try to speed things up. Baby walkers of the push-along kind allow the child to retain a normal walking position and let them experience the balance required in walking. The sit-in kind of walker doesn't promote the development of balance to the same extent and children may lean back or propel the walker on tiptoe, adopting an unhelpful position. Children love the mobility they allow and the fact that they are in the upright position but perhaps they shouldn't stay in the walker too long (Sonken and Stiff 1991).

Figure 2.1
Construction on a
small scale

Figure 2.2 Construction on a large scale – cooperating and learning about balance

Pretend and sociodramatic play

This is also known as symbolic play, fantasy or make believe play. Between two and three years old, children are just beginning to pretend. Their experience of the world has grown, allowing them to see more possibilities for play. They are beginning to imitate. However pretend play at this stage tends to be solitary because the children don't yet have the communication skills to share their experiences, which may indeed be very different to those of another child. And so children may prefer to play alone, perhaps inventing stories around a doll's family in a doll's house (Figure 2.3).

Other children may find empathising, i.e. understanding the feelings which arise from the play experience, problematic. Having to wait, to take turns, to share resources, to understand what other children are doing and know why they are doing it are all quite difficult competences for some children. As experiences multiply however, and this capacity for empathising develops, pretend play becomes important in the achievement of abstract thought (the children are doing something which represents or is symbolic of something else which is not present and so has to be visualised/imagined). This is a higher-level intellectual skill, which becomes possible when the children no longer need concrete props to aid their learning.

At the start of pretend play, children are more comfortable with realistic objects such as ballet shoes and tutus or masks and robots, while later, at around six years plus, the children's play themes are likely to show more diversity if they have materials which don't limit them to any specific development. While the younger group would

Figure 2.3
Construction on a
small scale –
practising fine motor
skills at the midline
of the body

probably need a fireman's hat or a hose to stimulate a 'fireman game', the older ones will form the idea from building up cardboard boxes to make a fire engine, a spaceship, a rocket, a double-decker bus or a magic cave and enjoy rustling around in boxes of junk to find materials which will adapt to and elaborate their theme. And so, while things like nurses' uniforms are fine for the smallest children, because they learn all about hospitals and what they are really like, such 'costumes' are not as likely to stimulate the older children to engage in lively pretend play. Lengths of colourful material or lacy curtains, with Velcro to help fastenings, just might.

Playing together

As these imaginative games develop, the children need someone to play with, and this 'someone' is usually chosen because they can enter into the spirit of the game – rather than for any personal feature. In the duo, trio or group there develops a shared understanding of what is going on, with, it appears, little need for conversation. The children read each other's non-verbal cues, their signals that spell out delight or dismay, agreement or argument, pleasure or pain. This kind of development can also stimulate linguistic development if the children share their ideas and explain to each other their thoughts, reasons and evaluations of what has gone on, i.e. the play process. It is not difficult to realise that children who have experienced the same sorts of things at home and who have the same value systems are more likely to blend together than children from different cultures. This can be helped if they share experiences in the earliest years so that they have a common repertoire to draw upon at play. Play can be more spontaneous if all the children can relate easily to the process that unfolds.

But what of the children with special needs?

Many children find this shift into another person's world very difficult and other children may shy away if the recipient doesn't seem to understand (by giving the 'wrong' non-verbal cues), avoiding eye contact or not seeming to want to take the conversation further. Some children seem unable to read the intentions of others, especially when only subtle differences in tone, rate of speech or facial expressions cause the meaning inherent in the communication to change. For children who appear to have significant difficulties, Chapter 3 on Asperger's syndrome and autism should provide some help.

How can children who find this change difficult be helped?

Children's pretend games are stimulated by their imaginations which feed, to begin with at least, on their real experiences. But so often when we think we are giving children a new experience, for example when taking them out, we don't really explain what it is all about. Think of popping children in the back seat of the car – do we explain where we are going in terms of passing a castle or even just 'going the same way down . . . St. and then we'll turn right down by the river . . .'? Or do we concentrate on driving and hope the children won't make a noise? Perhaps opportunities like this could build up the children's repertoire of experiences. Similarly expanding on 'something seen' could help develop children's understanding of other people's feelings (empathy) and their willingness to help others at some cost to themselves (altruism). Perhaps setting a hypothetical 'scene', explaining different reactions and asking children which they thought was the best way to respond could be salutary.

Example of 'a scene for discussion'

A new boy, Tom came to school and he trailed around looking miserable and was grumpy when other boys tried to make friends. He was rather untidy and wouldn't answer when some of the children asked, 'Where do you live?' A few days later it was Jack's birthday and his mum said he could invite anyone he wanted to tea, but to limit the number to six, because there was going to be time on the go-carts and there were only six available. Who should Jack invite?

This kind of story, based in the children's own experiences, can stimulate discussions, allowing different children to give their point of view. Without apportioning blame or praise, the teacher can 'summarise and discuss' – the final point being that there are usually pros and cons to be carefully considered and knowing something of the context is helpful in making the best decisions. Hopefully some children will want Tom to be there.

Perhaps seeing a fire engine or an ambulance or a police car or having a story or poem about one of them could instigate conversations about the *feelings* of the people involved rather than only the 'real' things such as going to hospital or having to be bandaged – or whatever these literal happenings might be. How for example does the fireman feel as he approaches a burning building? What does he think about? Is he always brave? This could lead to discussions about times when the children themselves have to be brave and it might just lead to a conclusion that boys should be able to cry, thus helping boys who do.

Another way in which staff at nursery or school could help, would be to build possible play materials around the interests of the children with special needs. This would mean that they could join in more easily, even instigate some of the play moves because they understood the nuances of what was going on. It would help their self-esteem tremendously if they could realise that some of the other children were joining in their game, for a sense of ownership can be tremendously rewarding.

With the older children who build more sophisticated play topics, a sensitive teacher can assign roles, giving the children who are operating at the lower end of the play development continuum and finding the complex play confusing, 'real' things to do, such as ticking a clipboard to show how many patients come into Accident and Emergency. To be able to fulfil such tasks they have to watch the more imaginative play and see how children are portraying different roles within it, while playing a significant part themselves. Children left out will withdraw further from the play, or through frustration they will cause some disruption to spoil it. Neither of these understandable reactions helps the children's development at all. They just learn how not to learn.

House corner

Such familiar settings give children the opportunity to take on the role of significant others in their lives and this is a good beginning for children who find it difficult to play. They have grown up with examples of different roles and it can be fascinating to watch them begin to show how other people feel and how facial expressions belong to a certain role, for example the mum or teacher in charge who looks cross. Observations of children and the poses they associate with different characters provide fascinating insights, perhaps demonstrating influences that lead to gender bias. Of course this is complex and influences outside the home have to be considered too. One six-year-old insisted that all nurses were 'ladies' despite having one for a dad!

And so, staff can stimulate pretend play at the correct level of demand by doing different things. They can:

- provide time, opportunities and the amount of space which makes imaginative play possible;
- guide the composition of groups so that children can learn from each other;
- tell lots of stories and poems (see Chapter 5) and show videos which have clear imaginative content. Above all, they can discuss the feelings of the characters to help the development of empathy. This helps them to be more sympathetic and perceptive.

In this kind of play the children are depending less on the development of their motor skills but they need to show a greater level of development in their emotional and linguistic skills. The kind of play that challenges their intellectual skills perhaps more than the others do is 'games with rules'.

Games with rules

From the very beginning of playing, children are learning about rules which relate to other aspects of their development. In the old favourite peek-a-boo, the baby soon learns about taking turns and when these are accompanied by nods and laughs, the reciprocity and turn taking in language is established. Some 'rules' are a little harder to understand. Think of the child playing hide and seek who believes he is hidden when he hides his eyes, or the one who runs back to hide in exactly the spot where she was discovered a moment ago. These are developmental stages in learning rules because they are mainly learned by imitation. Did anyone ever explain to you how to play games like this? This may well explain the difficulties of children who find it hard to understand what others are doing. If no one tells them, how are they to discover the rules of the game?

Simple games

By age five to six, the spontaneous games of early childhood are beginning to disappear and board games and team games take their place. Many children are skilled chess players and others modify the rules to suit themselves – sometimes without informing their opponent, which causes ructions!

As they do this, a new language of winning and losing, of cheating and competitiveness emerges. Now there are winning moves which can be practised, with the goal of outwitting an opponent. The goal is a tangible one of points scored and turns won. Certainly learning rather than practice is at the forefront of the activity. Is this still play? It is not difficult to see why this type of play comes last in the developmental stakes and to understand why children with special needs might not wish to join in at all.

Children in wheelchairs

Other children often find it easier to relate to children in wheelchairs than to children whose conversation is erratic or who 'can't do' lots of things when there is no obvious reason why this should be so. Explanations such as 'Jack's legs aren't very strong and so he needs a bit of help to get around' are accepted quickly and many children have an instinctive understanding of how they could help and are keen to do so. This means that there are fewer barriers to the children being included in play, in fact children often find ways to adapt the play scenario to let wheelchair bound children play an important part.

Example

Peter, aged seven, explained,

> We play Kings and Queens a lot because Jack has a real throne and he is in charge, telling us what to do. He orders us knights about and we have to go back and tell him if we've won the battle. Helen's a peasant and she waits around in case the King needs food or that ... Once we made a big procession and some of us hid behind Jack's chair and then jumped out of the sheet we had covered it with ... and we get turns to push Jack to the dinner hall and then we get first in the queue ...

The staff had played their part in easing Jack into the children's play by introducing games with balloons, for Jack had enough leg strength to kick them as he sat in his chair. He could also enjoy batting the balloons into the air because the slower pace meant he could manoeuvre his chair to retrieve them. Thus he was actively involved with the others in an enjoyable game. Later when a ball was substituted he became the 'ref' and kept the score.

But what of the children who find the wheelchair strange and avoid going near the child? One teacher made the wheelchair a 'magic chair' where children could sit for a moment to tell their news. (The real occupant was able to sit on a large beanbag for a spell.) The children loved this and it demystified the chair – in fact some children were reluctant to get out! Sometimes she covered it with a gold cloth and then stories about travelling to other lands (just like the magic carpet) or jingles were used to stimulate the children's imaginations. One such jingle was,

Flying away, flying away,
Please tell us,
Where shall we go today?
Over the rainbow and into the sky,
Flying, flying ever so high?

Look down on the icebergs and shiver with cold,
Look down to the sea and the sand, brightly gold,
Look down to the houses and people so small,
We're flying, we're flying
Up over them all!

We have a chair and it's magic you see,
And it takes us wherever we'd like to be,
So sometimes we travel all night and all day,
But then we land safely, all ready to play!

C. M.

And so, depending on the personality of the child and the inventiveness of the staff and the children, the wheelchair can become an asset to the classroom just as the child can.

CHAPTER 3

An introduction to conditions causing special needs and how difficulties may be helped through play

Due to the current policy on inclusion, many more children with a greater degree of special needs are coming into mainstream settings (Clough and Corbett 2000). This chapter provides an introduction to some of these special needs conditions, which I hope does not over-simplify or minimise the difficulties which children with any of these conditions face. Instead I hope this will encourage readers to find out more because each condition is complex and the implications of having such difficulties impact on every aspect of the children's lives. Appendix 5 offers a list of contact agencies to show where parents and professionals who wish to know more may obtain further advice and help.

To some extent the need for this extra information may depend on the type and level of difficulties the children exhibit. Behaviour difficulties that cause children to hurt others are always difficult, especially if there is no auxiliary help. Other conditions that are not disruptive to the routine of the day may be easier to cope with, but many professionals in school worry that they do not have the specialised training to understand and so help the children in their care. Many parents are also concerned that their children may not be able to have enough of the one-to-one attention which would help most, as the staff have to deal with many organisational and management duties as well as teaching the other children who have a whole range of abilities and difficulties too. This is very understandable and parents may well wonder how the staff can cope with their children with special needs who do need lots of care and attention if they are to fulfil their potential. Sometimes they will want to assist perhaps through offering practical advice on strategies that work at home and this is tremendously helpful, as after all they are the ones who know their children best. Other parents may sometimes appear resentful that not enough is being done. However, this can often be explained by their tiredness and constant anxiety resulting from waiting months or even years for a diagnosis or referral from their GP.

Perhaps the solution would be to involve 'outside' professionals to a greater degree? Unfortunately this doesn't look likely to happen. Why not? Consider paediatricians for example. Keen (2001) explains that since 1990 there has been an

80 per cent increase in the number of children presenting for special help. 'The services cannot cope,' she says, 'teachers, nursery nurses, support for learning teachers and classroom assistants will just have to do their best!' And of course they will. Having said that, where other professionals have been able to contribute, whether they are psychologists, physiotherapists, occupational or speech therapists, by working with the children and advising the teachers and parents, the children have benefited significantly from this level of support. It is always worth asking for access to these specialists and one way to make the most of the first meeting is to present a careful record of the child's difficulties in the context of the school as 'evidence of need'. If field notes are gathered from day one, the record can be full of pertinent information by the time any appointment comes round. If such details are not available, the school may be asked to collect them and the treatment programme could be delayed.

There can however be 'downsides' to any programme of therapy. Often, even usually, the exercises have to be practised at home after school when the children are tired and families have other demands. If everyone gets cross and the routine becomes tedious or associated with more failure, it becomes understandably easy to 'Let it go for today and we'll start again tomorrow.' This is the reason why some parents wish therapy could be incorporated into a programme of activities at school. If the therapy is primarily to help socialisation, this could be done through drama-type activities such as sociodramatic play where the meanings and strategies of social interactions could be explained, for example why the 'angry Giant' shows his anger by stamping his feet and wringing his hands, because children who don't really understand non-verbal behaviour may wonder why he does. The stamping may not seem a logical thing to do at all! However, if movement learning difficulties are the stumbling block, daily perceptual–motor programmes can help through giving lots of regular supervised practice of activities to develop coordination and balance, i.e. movement abilities. But of course this strategy isn't easy to organise or sustain if the children need one-to-one supervision to be safe. (For details of a video showing six- and seven-year-old children taking part in a perceptual–motor programme see Appendix 5 under 'Dyspraxia'.)

These kinds of interventions however, ideally with physiotherapist support, do prevent the children being taken out of school, missing lessons and even more importantly being seen as 'different'. Sometimes not understanding 'what the difference is' can make children uneasy, especially if the affected children look just the same as themselves. A broken arm is easy to understand and talk about, but difficulties with perception and communication would be beyond the understanding of most early years' children. Moreover, there is the ethical question of explaining one child's difficulties to another, especially when these problems may be ameliorated over time.

Another set of problems can arise when questions such as 'Who is teaching the children with special needs?' are asked, for teachers who are wonderful with 'ordinary' children may not be so good with children with special needs. Perhaps the assumption that they will be, needs to be examined, so that the placing of children achieves the best results. Teachers and other staff may well need extra help and training to understand the children's difficulties. Parents and the school management team need to discover if this is the case and take appropriate steps. Parents could offer to help by meeting the staff and explaining the difficulties the children face at home. If, as one example, the staff learn that getting dressed is an exhausting and frustrating business, they will understand the children's tiredness or their unwillingness to take their clothes off again as soon as they arrive if PE comes early in the day. As a first step, school managers could ensure that the teachers have access to help. Communication and cooperation between all of the carers is vital if the children are to flourish.

It is possible that providing the most appropriate help in school could be eased if children had a specific condition or a 'label' which spelt out their difficulties, for then the details could be studied and teaching strategies developed to suit. This could also provide a ready means of communication between school and home. In some areas, especially if the child is a 'typical' case, then that does happen. The trouble is that there are few children who are textbook cases, showing all of the symptoms of a condition at some recognised level of severity. The borderlines between conditions, even between those that have and do not have the condition, are blurred. This makes identification, assessment and planning for teaching very difficult.

The medical profession must have the same problem, because lots of parents tell of their children with ostensibly the same difficulties being given different diagnoses depending on who gives the advice. The question is whether the diagnosticians tend to 'see' their particular specialism. Certainly, when classroom teachers are asked about a child's difficulties, they are likely to diagnose dyslexia. Research carried out in 59 primary schools in 10 regions (Croll and Moses 1995) showed that teachers almost always equated learning difficulties with reading and writing problems, assumed the difficulty was dyslexia and considered the cause lay in attributes in the children themselves rather than any reading programme or other school factors. Few identified movement learning difficulties. On the other hand, physiotherapists and occupational therapists seeing the same demonstrated problems are likely to diagnose dyspraxia, movement learning difficulties, while paediatricians may 'see' attention deficit disorder (ADD) with or without the 'H' for hyperactivity.

How can this be? It would seem inexplicable until one recognises the overlap of symptoms (Figure 3.1) which make diagnosis difficult; the sad realisation that one child may have two separate conditions which overlap, such as Asperger's syndrome and ADD; the fact that at assessment the child may be having a particularly good or bad day thus masking the true picture; and the reality that some parents find discussing their child's problems with a stranger overwhelmingly difficult and so inadvertently over or under state the symptoms. All of these may well hinder an accurate diagnosis.

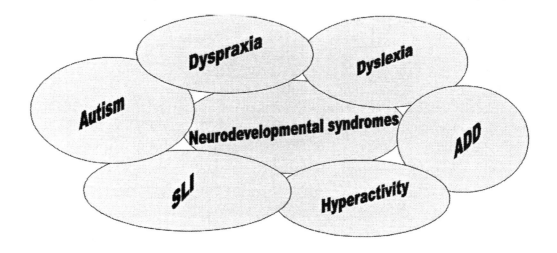

Figure 3.1 Comorbidity: the overlap of symptoms

The conditions outlined in this chapter are all complex and this text can only give an introduction in the hope that readers will be stimulated to find out more. These conditions or aspects of them are presenting in mainstream education now, so help must depend on understanding the manifestations of the difficulties in the classroom and playground settings. The playground is mentioned because children who are different in any way, by being the biggest, smallest, cleverest, having glasses, not being able to do whatever, may well be targeted by bullies. This of course adds hugely to the distress children with special needs feel, as they are likely to be even more vulnerable than other children if they do not understand ways to cope with it all (see Chapter 4).

Above all, the staff must understand that children are not being intentionally disruptive or aggressive or withdrawn or clumsy. These characteristics are all part of the condition(s) they have. The most helpful thing is for those of us who are lucky enough not to have these difficulties to try to see the world through the eyes of the children who do. For only in this way can we begin to understand the problems that some children will have, not for a day or a year, but very possibly for always.

Let's look more closely at some of the conditions now, i.e. Asperger's syndrome and autism, dyspraxia, dyslexia, Down's syndrome and ADD/ADHD, always remembering that individual children may present with only some of the difficulties at different levels of severity. They may also have aspects of more than one condition so observation, identification and assessment must focus on what the child is able to do, rather than being biased by any label they have been given. The good news is that, with the appropriate assistance, many of these children can improve. Things do get better. Maturation and the experiences gained by living and learning do help, along with the fact that as children grow they are able to make choices. This allows them to concentrate on and get praise for the things they can do. 'Although there is no "cure", the label need not stick' (Caan 1998).

Asperger's syndrome

Example 1

Jack is eight years old. He was diagnosed as having Asperger's syndrome at two years of age. Unfortunately he had to move from the school where the staff had come to understand his condition and were tolerant when they realised Jack couldn't help his outbursts and his occasional aggressive behaviour. How did the first day at his new school go? Listen to his mum.

> Last week Jack started at a new school. He was desperately anxious to go, but as we got ready he started rocking, backwards and forwards, heel to toe. This is a sure sign that he is tense. However, he approached the classroom quietly and sat down at his place without fuss – we had gone over and over what he should do before we left home. Earlier in the week I went into school to try to explain Jack's difficulties, to pave the way as it were. The class teacher was very interested, although she explained that she didn't know much about Asperger's. She suggested that on the first day I should stay for a short time to settle him. So I sat just outside the classroom with my fingers crossed that all would be well. I had just begun to relax when, in the midst of the teacher introducing him to the other children, Jack blurted out, 'What bus goes past here? I know all the routes – I know where the 10 goes and the 16, I do, I do. I do.' He ran to the window, for although the others hadn't heard a bus approach, Jack had and the need to add to his already tremendous store of knowledge about bus routes took over. He didn't mean to disrupt the class, in fact he was completely unaware that he had done so. He also ignored two children who were offering him information about the local buses and he was totally oblivious to their reaction and those of the other children in the class who were aghast at his behaviour. They wouldn't have dreamed of getting out of their seats and interrupting the teacher. Suddenly, the atmosphere in the room changed; it seemed as if it had become harder to welcome this new boy into their class. It just took that one episode, but slowly and almost imperceptibly, the children seemed to withdraw, unsure of what to make of Jack's unusual behaviour.

Mum explained that she was in despair, although she had anticipated that something like this could happen. She had rehearsed the expected routine of going into the class and settling down quietly, but she couldn't begin to cover all possibilities of the things Jack might do. And yet she knew he didn't mean to cause any harm. He wanted a friend but didn't understand the way to make one.

Example 2

Another child with Asperger's syndrome, Leah aged seven, was walking home through the park when she came across a toddler struggling to get out of his buggy. His mum was standing chatting to a friend nearby. 'The baby wanted to come with me – he held out his hands and clung to me,' explained Leah, 'so I took him out and we went for a walk.' Almost immediately the frantic mum was in full cry behind her and Leah was marched home, terrified but not really understanding why. Leah had no intention of doing anything wrong. She couldn't understand the reaction, to what to her, was a logical thing to do. The child was unhappy and wanted to go with her, so why not? Leah certainly couldn't understand why.

These brief scenarios highlight the main features of Asperger's syndrome, listed by Burgoine and Wing (1983) as:

- lack of empathy (i.e. lack of understanding other people's perceptions of events and reactions to them);
- naive, inappropriate, one-sided interactions (i.e. constant trivial talk without pausing to gauge reactions or to allow interruptions);
- little or no ability to form friendships (possibly because of no understanding of give and take);
- pedantic repetitive speech;
- poor non-verbal communication (parents explain that they have to over-react in making gestures and facial expressions if meaning is to be transmitted);
- intense absorption in certain subjects (i.e. a compulsion to amass facts – maps or train timetables or the names of cars);
- clumsy, ill-coordinated movement and odd postures.

Other researchers have compiled different criteria and there does not seem to be one list that pleases everyone. My own explanations are in the brackets that follow the criteria set by Burgoine and Wing.

Yet the story is not all gloom. There are favourable sides to Asperger's too. Many children can be content with their own company and relish the time spent following their own interests which would be denied them if they always had to fit in with what others wanted to do. They often have a good long-term memory stretching back days, which would normally be beyond recall and good observational skills, i.e. a good eye for detail. Further, if their obsessional behaviour can be channelled into commitment to discovering things, for example in a research field, then these children come to realise that career success can stem from their condition. Then obsession becomes commitment to the job at hand.

How many children are affected?

The number given by Ehlers and Gillberg (1993) is that Asperger's syndrome appears in 1:300 children, while autism affects 1:1,000. Some children have a dual diagnosis, i.e. they show traits of each condition.

How are the difficulties recognised in children?

The condition can be suspected through watching children play and noting if and how they join in, whether and to what extent they will share or take turns when it is the correct social thing to do. Such assessments concern the quality of reciprocity. A key point for observation is whether the children can hold, even bear, eye-contact and to what extent they protect their personal space from intrusion by others. If the suspicion is confirmed, parents may be asked about their child's willingness/ reluctance to make friends and how they cope with peer pressure and competition. Then there are observations about the children's speech. Very often the children with Asperger's are only marginally late in acquiring speech according to developmental norms, but their speech patterns are strange; incessant questioning and one-sided conversations on topics not related to the activity going on at the time, are common features which raise alarms. The children may have a strange tone of voice and use precise clipped language, which makes them stand out from the others. And all of this while using an extensive vocabulary. The final diagnosis will involve psychological tests to find the child's level of understanding as to how others perceive the world.

Movement patterns are also checked as clumsiness is one characteristic common to children with Asperger's. Information is also gathered on the children's interests and to what extent they could be seen as obsessive.

What can be done through play?

Attwood (1998) suggests that parents should become their child's best friend and as such practise the games that children of their child's age are playing. This is so that the children learn the technical things about the play, such as how to build a road in the sand or how to play ball in the yard — whatever the current fad is. The parents can also help the children to appreciate possible reactions that a friend might have, for example 'You tell David what to do and then let him suggest what you should do — or he will be sad.' This helps understanding about the social side of the play. The thing is that the child with Asperger's may not recognise the expressions of sadness or gladness their playmates show. These have to be taught through lots of activities recognising smiley faces, drawing sad faces, discussing what would make someone sad, lessons which cover aspects of learning which most children acquire naturally and without such painstaking input.

A last facet to mention is the child with Asperger's preference for a strict routine, possibly because expectations and events can be pre-planned thus preventing the necessity for unforeseen responses. Having to respond all day long causes stress and tension as Naomi explains in her poem.

Go

Go, Go Go,
Let me be,
I am not sad or strange,
I am free.

I do not understand
What makes you laugh or cry,
I am lonely when I'm with you
So Goodbye.

Naomi, aged 16

What are the differences between Asperger's syndrome and autism?

Adults often ask about the differences between these two conditions and it is important to outline them to give a picture of the extent of the difficulties which children with each experience.

Asperger's syndrome ——————— autism

These two conditions have different places on the autistic spectrum. They have common features but children with Asperger's tend to be less isolated; they try to make friends even though when that possibility arises they have difficulty in knowing how to sustain any interaction. Moreover the children with Asperger's do not have the accompanying intellectual or learning difficulties, which compound the problems of autism. Children who have autism show a greater degree of isolation through lack of responsiveness and severe language impairment. The classic autistic child is silent and aloof (Attwood 1998).

How can they be helped through play?

The Son-rise programme of therapy for children with autism advises a lengthy daily spell of uninterrupted and private play, so that no distractions can mar any opportunity to establish communication (Figure 3.2). Parents of the more severely affected children are advised to be full of energy and enthusiasm, to mimic their child's actions, even their obsessive behaviour and/or echolalia (senseless repetition of words). The hope is that the child will recognise these actions and through the shared experience a window for communication will emerge.

Figure 3.2 Teacher and child playing peep-boo to encourage child to hold gaze

(For places to get help see Appendix 5.)

Dyspraxia

Listen to Sarah aged seven telling what it's like to have dyspraxia.

Example

Sarah explains:

> I don't like having dyspraxia because it makes me fall over some of the time and I get sore knees. I can't do gym very well at least the gym that they do but I can do lots of things they can't. Sometimes I can fly! But no one picks me to be in their team and that makes me cry because they don't think I can play. And I forget things and people get cross. I'm not very good at writing but my teacher says I have a wonderful imagination and when she has time, she writes out my stories and puts them on the wall and that's really good. One horrid boy said I was stupid to have to get her to write for me. Is that true?
>
> I don't really like going out much because it's too noisy. We went to the cinema to see Harry Potter but I couldn't hear what was said because everyone

around had popcorn and was wriggling around too much. I don't like school either, because my teacher has left and the new one shouts when I forget to go to the toilet and sometimes she won't let me out. I'm not sure who will be my friend. I don't want anyone who holds my hand too tight because that really hurts. It makes me cry... but I do want a special friend.

From this brief description the elements of dyspraxia, as outlined next, stand out.

Poor balance and coordination

This means that movements are clumsy and the day holds many spills. There are many symptoms, but one of the most common is poor muscle tone. Lax muscles failing to hold the joints secure means that actions lack control. This can affect gross movements – which involve the large muscle groups, so that actions like walking and running, i.e. all the basic movement patterns, are poorly executed – or fine motor skills which means that actions such as writing, drawing, cutting and spreading are difficult. If muscles in the mouth are affected (verbal dyspraxia), then poor articulation may make speech incomprehensible, although the child understands and makes the correct responses showing that comprehension is not affected. For the same reason, eating can be messy with lots of spills and dribbles. Children chew with their mouths open because the closed-mouth chewing action is ineffective. This slows everything down and can also be socially unacceptable and lead to children not being invited to parties, so it is socially isolating too.

Poor short-term memory

The children need constant reminders of what they have to do or where they have to go. Little awareness of the passing of time means that children with dyspraxia are often late. They are constantly chivvied to 'Hurry up' and often mums and dads will do too much for them just to get there in time. The children may be left feeling inadequate and confused, although relieved to have escaped the movement task.

Difficulty in retaining friends

This is because poor motor skills mean they cannot ride a bike, swim or play football at the level of skill expected for their age group, so that when friends go off to play they are left out which is extremely hurtful. Moreover, movement skills are public, everyone immediately sees when children cannot skip or get dressed quickly or remember what to do next. Humiliation is often the name of the game.

Poor planning and organisational skills

Many of these children generally have trouble getting themselves and their 'resources' such as schoolbags, jackets, lunch boxes and bus tickets to the right place at the right time. This could be due to their poor short-term memory as they forget the routines that have been successful the day before. They do this with other school learning too, for example with sums, where success one day doesn't mean that the child will remember how to do them the next. This causes lots of frustration to parents and teachers as well as to the children themselves. And so these often very bright children land in the bottom group in class doing their self-esteem no good at all.

Inability to work at the midline

Many children with dyspraxia find it extremely difficult to complete tasks that ask them to cope at, near or crossing over the midline of the body. This may be because they are late to develop a sense of hand dominance. These activities are many and varied, such as using a knife and fork, opening a jar – in fact any action where the hands have to cooperate to achieve something while doing different things at the same time. Writing comes into this category because one hand has to steady the paper as the other makes the symbols. This is why there is nearly always a discrepancy between the quality of the children's oral and written work. Letting the child use a computer can be very helpful as the hands work on their own side of the body.

Average or above average intelligence

These tend to be bright children. There is usually a discrepancy between the children's intellectual IQ and their performance IQ as measured by their success in motor tasks. They do not have global developmental delay, although poor movement can affect all aspects of their development, even their personality if constant failure causes them to become isolated and withdrawn. They are hampered by their lack of motor ability, yet given time and support in scribing, and possibly in structuring their work (for they may have difficulty ordering their ideas), they can produce original work of high quality.

Good imaginations

Some children with dyspraxia have fantastic imaginations, but care has to be taken for these could lead them into danger.

Example

For a time Sarah believed she was a fairy and one day she was found eating berries 'because that's what fairies do'. She truly believed she could fly and had to be supervised every moment in case she decided to try. Of course such assertions met with derision from her schoolmates who told her she was 'a bit odd'. Sarah got lots of comfort in her dream world. Perhaps this explains why she would sit, apparently staring into space in the midst of lots of activity. When the planning and organising of the day got too much, she chilled out and escaped to her own more comfortable world.

Nonetheless the family was relieved to have a diagnosis of dyspraxia because they had feared something much worse and Sarah was so relieved to know that the fault was not hers. People began to realise that telling her to try harder was not appropriate because she was already trying as hard as she could. Her new teacher recognised her difficulties; the diagnosis meant that she was able to get a classroom assistant. The assistant helped Sarah by encouraging her to concentrate for longer and finish her work and so homework, which had caused great unhappiness, could be forgotten. Sarah's parents were so relieved that one huge struggle which had affected all the family had been overcome.

How many children are affected?

Current research claims that between 6 and 10 per cent of all children have some degree of dyspraxia. Boys feature in a ratio of 4:1 although when girls have it they seem to be more severely affected (Dyspraxia Foundation 1999). This means that there will be two or three children in every class – the ones who are never picked, who hate PE, who get lost going from place to place and who never get sent on an errand, 'because they'd never come back' (teacher's comment).

How are these difficulties recognised in children?

One of the earliest signs is poor muscle tone – babies who are floppy and because of this lack of muscle strength, reach their motor milestones late – just within the 'limits of normal development' (Ayres 1972). Few children with dyspraxia have managed to crawl. Why? Because the messages which should pass from the cerebral cortex of the brain to each separate limb in turn, are somehow relayed to more than one which makes it impossible to know which arm or leg to move first. And so these children lack early sequencing practice, which may impinge on learning activities which require this skill, such as reading and storytelling. The children also miss the opportunity to learn about balance while they are in a safe, prone position close to the ground and how adjustments have to be made to cope with uneven floors or obstacles which lie in their path. They also lose early learning about distance and direction, for example how far to stretch out and where to reach, perhaps to retrieve a toy. And so from toddlerhood on, they find movement learning difficult. Many need intensive programmes of physiotherapy to strengthen their limbs, but it is not always possible to obtain this through the NHS for those who are less severely affected and private therapy can be very expensive, putting it out of the reach of many families. Unfortunately this lack of muscle strength can mean that the children can't always control their movements. They tend to bump and barge without intending to, but still find the recipients get annoyed. One perplexed teacher explained, 'You'll know the child with dyspraxia – very untidy, very lovable and always standing on your feet!' Safety is a constant worry, because children going too fast may not be able to stop at the kerb. Parents tell of being anxious for their safety every moment of the day.

Some children with dyspraxia wander around, not knowing what to do, or play in a desultory fashion, not really achieving very much. This may be caused by their poor planning skills and those who try to help have to observe till they are sure where their difficulty lies before intervening. It is easy to think a child can't do a particular movement and teach that, when the real problem lies in the planning and organising, not really the doing at all.

What can be done to help the children through play?

Outdoor play on large apparatus

One of the best environments for observation and assessment of children, is when they play out of doors on large apparatus. So that children are not afraid and know they will be safe, the pieces of apparatus should be well spaced out (Figure 3.3). This means that approach runs do not cross and that children tackling an activity are not rushed by someone coming up behind them. It is important that different levels of challenge are offered and that the children are free to select because most will know what they are able to do.

Figure 3.3 Arrangement of apparatus outdoors

It should be noted that some children with dyspraxia will not know their own strengths and limitations and have to be closely and carefully supervised. This is easiest if there are not too many children on the apparatus at once.

Indoor play with large and small apparatus

If weather is inclement or there is no safe outdoor play area, apparatus indoors can suffice. The spinning cone (Figure 3.4) is especially good for children with

Figure 3.4 Making backs lead the action

dyspraxia because they often have little awareness of their backs. 'Making the cone spin' is one of the few 'good fun' activities where the back leads the action and this helps the children feel each part of their back, especially if they slow down the cone and make it spin the other way.

Estimating distances such as 'How many steps do you think you will need to cross the (rope) river?' is a good game because trying out and counting the steps gives immediate feedback (Figure 3.5). Walking heel-to-toe also holds quite a difficult balance challenge and is a useful observational tool for noting retained reflexes (Goddard 1996).

Figure 3.5 Careful stepping to what is there already

Indoor climbing frames do take up space but they can quickly become a castle or when covered, a hidey hole where children can have some peace and quiet. This helps lots of children with all kinds of special needs become calm and ready to join in again.

Many of the early years' classroom/nursery activities help the development of fine motor skills. Sometimes people forget that a good sense of balance helps fine motor skills too. Fun activities such as trying to balance a plastic plate – as part of a circus theme – let children become aware of the constant adjustment that is needed to balance well (Figure 3.6). Sometimes jingles can add to the sense of fun and achievement – even keep the children trying when frustration threatens to set in. One could be:

> Spin the plate now,
> Spin the plate now,
> Keep it twirling up high,
> Watch it so closely.
> Push the stick to the sky.

Figure 3.6 Learning about balance and distance

Keep it spinning,
Keep it spinning,
Watch it go round,
Then toss it and catch it
Before it hits the ground!

C.M.

Threading beads is a good aiming exercise, which happens at the midline of the body – a place where dyspraxic children find it difficult to work. It would help these children if staff would speak about the fundamental action involved in an activity (in this case 'aiming straight forward with just a little push') as well as the outcome (the pattern made by the beads or the pleasure they gives when they can be worn).

Dressing and undressing a doll give lots of practice at the fiddly jobs like doing up buttons, while the ordering of 'what comes off or goes on next' helps children with poor planning skills, for there is a sequence of activities which needs to happen if the doll is to be dressed correctly. This should transfer to helping the children's own dressing skills.

All of this motor learning can happen through play without adding stress to the children's day.

Dyslexia

Some of the main difficulties children with dyslexia have are in spelling, reading and writing. It is not difficult to see why the children's education is hampered because reading permeates into most areas of the curriculum and even into some leisure activities, such as being able to read the side-of-the-pool instructions when swimming, understanding the instructions on a board game or construction kits, or for the older child, finding directions around town. Computers have graphics which help, but many other activities need some skill in reading, which means decoding and understanding the meaning of the print. Children who have dyslexia find this a difficult thing to do.

The difficulties children with dyslexia have, can be subdivided into:

- phonological difficulties
- decoding difficulties
- spelling difficulties
- poor short- and long-term memory
- slow processing of information
- difficulty automising information
- handwriting problems
- visual difficulties
- poor movement skills.

Of course, not all children have all these difficulties and each can be at a different level of severity.

What is involved in being able to read and spell?

Many researchers agree that a certain level of phonological skill is necessary for reading. That means the children must be able to recognise each letter and associate it with the sound it makes. If this is indeed the root skill within reading, then it would seem that work on phonics should precede reading text, for as the children develop competence in recognising letters, they are also learning to match the sounds they hear to the symbols, i.e. the letters they see. And of course phonological skill means more than recognising discrete sounds. Children gradually learn a number of blends, which give them access to syllables and the rhythm of words. These are important steps towards reading fluently.

Other researchers prefer a different approach. They advise 'exposure to print' as a first encounter. This is a less analytic way of being introduced to the written word. They suggest that having children follow stories that are being read to them helps them to realise that the written words correspond to those that are spoken in a more meaningful way. They claim that this method also promotes a love of stories, so that reading becomes a pleasurable experience. In this mode, children become familiar with the structure of stories too, learning how a story unfolds and the logic of a sequence of events. Stories are also good for developing memories and this would be particularly beneficial if this aspect of dyslexia was one that needed help. Parents know their children's angry responses when, trying to hurry through a story they have told endless times before, they omit one part. The children immediately tell them the exact words that have been 'forgotten'. And if favourite books have just a few words on a page, some very young children can even point to the exact word that has been missed out. This explains why some children have word recognition skills beyond their phonological skills, i.e. they recognise words they can't sound out. Can you see how different experiences contribute to the children's ability to read?

Both of these pre-reading skills are very important, because comprehension, i.e. understanding the meaning within the words, appears to develop from exposure to these sub skills – phonic awareness, syllabification (i.e. recognising the sound of just one part of a word) and the relationship between sound and symbol (Reid 1996). And whereas in the past, research has queried whether one way was more successful for poor readers than the other, today both strategies come together and the mix is adjusted to suit each child. This makes sense, because learning to recognise words by sight and being able to sound out unfamiliar words are complementary, not opposing processes.

But despite a blend of methods, some children still find reading very difficult. What can be amiss? There are several possibilities. First, the children who have difficulty decoding words may resort to guessing, for if they depend on visual reading without phonological skills what else is there for them to do? They may use familiar characteristics, like the initial letter that they recognise, and so they guess 'book' as 'ball' or they may consider the length of the word and guess 'church' as 'camera' because there are the same number of letters and the word takes up the same space on the page. Neither of these strategies is likely to be successful.

Second, as Stein (2000) explains, over 20 per cent of individual difficulties in literacy skill are down to visual motion sensitivity. If the eyes don't stabilise, the letters on the page appear to move around and their order becomes confused. Children talk of letters floating over the page or going blurry or moving over one another. And so 'visual magnocellar weakness may cause letter position confusions leading to fuzzy orthographic representation' (Stein 2000).

A further difficulty arises if the children pronounce words incorrectly, for then their auditory processing doesn't give the correct cues for phonological analysis (i.e. if they don't hear the sound correctly how can they sound it out?). This contributes to poor spelling, which in itself is a complex skill. When Peter, aged seven, retold the story of Goldilocks, he wrote, 'She nokd at the dorr but nobdi ansad the dorr because the bers went to klekt stics.' (She knocked at the door but nobody answered the door because the bears went to collect sticks.) From his rendering of 'dorr', can you tell where he lived? That spelling certainly reflected how he heard the word in his head. His story makes us wonder how phonetic our language is.

Children who find spelling difficult can often internalise one rule, such as 'i before e except after c' but only use it successfully when in the context of exercises which focus on that rule. When they become engrossed in story writing, other things become important and the spelling skill disappears. If spelling is overemphasised in these situations, soon children may limit their writing to using words they can spell. The result is dull, unimaginative prose and yet orally, these same children may be able to enchant listeners with an expressive, absorbing story.

How many children are affected?

The British Dyslexia Association (1999) claims that between 4 and 10 per cent of the population have severe difficulties with literacy, with boys featuring heavily in that group. These are likely to be bright children with a specific learning difficulty. The trouble is that children with dyslexia will shy away from experiences where they feel, or are made to feel, inadequate and so they restrict reading to 'when it has to be done', and rarely or never pick up a book for pleasure. Thus the cycle of disadvantage grows, because their classmates, fortunate not to experience these difficulties, are reading more and more. As this helps their fluency as well as their comprehension, the gap between those who can and cannot read widens.

One helpful strategy for those that find reading problematic is to have books with larger print and therefore fewer words on each page. This reduces the task so that children do not feel overwhelmed by the sight of the text they have to read even before they begin to try. This technique has been shown to help children with poor word processing skills because, with fewer words, there is more time for them to cope. A second strategy is that children learn to scan so that they do not have to identify every word on the page but identify only the key ones which convey the meaning of the text.

This slow processing of information can be accompanied by a difficulty in mastering automaticity – 'a learned process which consolidates the sub skills in reading, thus freeing up the memory processes to focus on variables other than the mechanics of reading' (Chasty 1990). Children with difficulties in reading may well have this problem and they need to be taken slowly and carefully through appropriate texts, with much repetition to give confidence and security and to ensure that the method is internalised. Over-learning is advised, as long as monotony and boredom are avoided. Decisions about how and when to introduce new material are difficult to make.

There also appears to be a gender difference in what children choose to read, although it is hard to say why more boys choose factual books than girls. Do girls sit longer on knees listening to fairy stories and go on to choose these kinds of stories for themselves? Are there cultural influences on the choice of books that appear at home? Do dads and mums intentionally choose 'boys books' for their sons? Perhaps books like *Bob the Builder* will go some way to reducing this gender bias or it may be that girls will not like these sorts of stories at all. There are always lots of questions to be answered.

How can dyslexic children be helped through play?

One approach which has been found to help slow readers is the multisensory approach. This means that all the information children take in from the environment through their senses (kinesthetic, visual, auditory and tactile) is utilised to provide reinforcement to the learning that is going on. And so as children 'read' a story they also hear it (Figure 3.7). Also they may well engage in sociodramatic play to 'feel' the meaning of the words, for example through reaching to the ceiling and feeling the pull of the movement as they stretch above them, the children would have another experience to add to the concept of stretching; they would learn a new directional word and so the idea of the stretch would be more likely to be retained.

Houston *et al.* (1996) explain that 'Children become aware of rhyme and alliteration before they go to school and this can significantly influence their eventual success in learning to read and spell.' And so in the nursery, nursery rhymes, made-up poems and jingles along with old-fashioned circle games can be

Figure 3.7 Multisensory learning

the stimulus for lots of fun. If these contribute to reading ability as well as teaching body/kinesthetic awareness that is a huge bonus. (Many examples appear in Chapter 5.)

An example could be:

Tapping

Tap on your shoulder, then tap on your nose,
Clap hands together and do you suppose
You could tap on two elbows and tap on two knees?
Then tap very gently wherever you please?
Clap hands together, 1, 2 and 3.
Stretch them right out as far as you see,
Now shake your left hand, then shake your right,
Shake both together with all of your might.
Give them a rest now and hide them away,
Are you ready to show them?
Do it, 'hooray!'

C.M.

Jingles like this allow emphasis on the quality of words and so the children come to appreciate their expressiveness. And if they are encouraged to act them out, they have a fun way of sustaining their interaction with the words, letting them dwell on both the sound and the meaning. And as they 'feel' the words, they are practising their motor control, for 'tap' must be gentle while 'clap' can be much stronger. Body awareness is also developed through the children recognising their body parts and knowing where they are.

(For lots more of these see Macintyre, C. *Early Intervention in Movement*, also published by David Fulton Publishers.)

And so, although there is no cure for dyslexia, there is much that can be done to help prevent the fall in self-esteem that was the fate of children before the condition was recognised and children's ability was gauged by what they read aloud and what they wrote. As with all other special needs, early identification of children's difficulties allows intervention. If this is done sympathetically through play activities, it need not go against the child-centred approach to learning, but can be built in to this method in a caring contextualised way.

Language difficulties or specific language impairment

The three terms which are used to describe this condition are specific language impairment (SLI), language delay and language disorder and although they are often used interchangeably, there are implicit differences which affect both learning and teaching.

The first of these, SLI, tells us that children have difficulties with comprehension (i.e. understanding language) or expression (i.e. being able to use language). They may have difficulty with one or both. Using these terms shows that the children do not have a global delay but that their difficulties are confined to the language aspect of their development. But of course, this means that they will have associated difficulties with communication and learning in every aspect of their lives.

The second and third terms highlight important differences between language delay and language disorder and these influence prognoses about the children's progress and indicate the kind of intervention that would be best. But how do we know which is which? Let's look at language delay first.

Language delay

As young children experiment with language, they make what seem to adults to be mistakes. They say, 'I go-ed to bed' or 'I wented to the park', but these are examples of the children experimenting with language forms that they have understood; they are trying out 'rules' because adding 'ed' puts a verb into the past tense, doesn't it? This is a natural part of promising language development. Most children do this and at the right age it is often charming, making adults smile. No one would think of being anxious. But when these 'mistakes' persist, when they continue to be made past the time when more mature forms of language should be appearing, then there is cause for some concern. If the children are progressing through the 'normal' developmental stages but just at a slower pace than is usual, they are said to have language delay. The delay may be short term or longer lasting and at different levels of severity, but once they do catch up their subsequent development of speech is normal in both sequence and pattern.

But of course, being able to converse involves much more than being able to use the correct grammatical rules and some children's language development is untypical and uneven. They have difficulties that would be classed as language disorders.

Language disorder

What then are the elements of language that cause difficulties? What do children need to learn to do? To be fluent, articulate speakers they have to:

- learn to listen and recognise speech sounds;
- learn how to make them (articulation);
- know the meaning of words (both received and spoken);
- be able to combine words into sentences;
- be able to vary the intonation so that words carry different meanings and be able to understand when others do this too;
- 'read' the non-verbal cues which influence the literal meaning of interactions.

This is an extensive list. Accurate identification of discrete causes of difficulty is best done by a speech and language therapist.

Children who can't make themselves understood need help as soon as possible because they become frustrated and unhappy, and because so much of language acquisition is taken for granted, families may be mystified by their child's inability to converse. Listen to Sean's dad talking about Sean's difficulties with articulation.

Possibly Sean's speech difficulties were caused by him having been without oxygen when he was born, although no one at the hospital would admit that. He was a breech birth and everything went wrong – so much so that he was kept on the 'at risk' register for a year. Needless to say we were frantic with worry and just so glad that he survived, that the possibility of any learning difficulties seemed really remote and unimportant. As he grew though, we did look out for developmental delays – but all seemed to be well. He was a good size and was a smiling, healthy baby. His difficulties didn't become apparent until Sean began to try to talk. He had done all the babbling that babies do at around a year, so we were surprised that when he started to try to communicate, his language just didn't make sense to us. He obviously knew what he meant, because when we asked him to repeat what he had said, we could recognise the same story, the same combination of sounds all over again. This made Sean very frustrated and he would get into a rage because we couldn't understand. He knew what we said – he smiled at the correct times and did what he was told and he enjoyed lots of stories, so we knew that comprehension was not a problem. This was solely in his articulation, but we could see the effect this was having on his confidence. He became clingy whenever new people appeared and we worried about how he would cope at school and so we pressed hard for speech therapy. Our GP said Sean would grow out of it, that all would be well, but we couldn't take that risk.

We had to wait some time and Sean was nearly four before we got help. The therapist told us that 'all his vowels and consonants were mixed up' and that his language was 'quite severely impaired' – which we realised. They stressed that this was primarily a motor problem affecting his control of the speech apparatus. Sean knew what he wanted to say, but he couldn't form the words. What concerned us, was what the specialists were going to do to help.

We were relieved that the help was to come in the form of games, i.e. through activities that could be experienced as play. Sean had first of all to learn a number of single sounds, concentrating on one per week and recognise where in his mouth these sounds were made. The first one was 't' and Sean went around the house practising 't' 't' 't', a sound made at the front of the mouth, until he was able to do it easily. One of his favourite games was to stand in the centre of a circle of pictures and as he said 't' he had to jump on a picture of something that started with that letter, such as a truck or telescope, and miss out other pictures (this game is illustrated in Figure 3.8).

This kind of input continued for about a year, the sounds changing all the time. 'Tell me a front sound' or 'Tell me a back sound' seemed a strange kind of conversation to be having with a four-year-old, but we kept the practice light-hearted and Sean enjoyed it. When he went to school, reading was easy because he already knew all of his sounds. This was a real bonus because it helped his confidence. Interestingly, his teacher said it was the first time a child had told her where sounds were made! He also was encouraged to blow bubbles or play blow football and suck through a straw – all sorts of fun exercises to strengthen the muscles in his mouth and so help his control.

Sean is now nine. Over the years there have been lots of times when his articulation has regressed. When he is tired he mumbles and he won't try to speak out in front of the class. He has lots of good ideas though and seems content to be a listener and a doer, which seems to be acceptable at school. When he is fresh and able to concentrate his speech is quite clear, although we still have to ask him to speak up and take time.

Figure 3.8 Speech therapy game

Cluttering

Taking time is a problem for children with a different speech difficulty called cluttering. This condition is suspected when the children's speech is rapid and becomes so muddled that it is difficult to discern any of what is being said. A child may start off at a relatively normal pace but then get faster and faster and be unable to slow down. The child may have breathing difficulties which hinder fluency and sometimes syllables of words are missed out altogether. Strangely enough the child can be unaware of this – however this lack of awareness does hinder the therapy. A physical abnormality may be responsible for this kind of speech and there may be a hereditary condition. Interestingly, fewer children with this difficulty seek help than do those who stutter – perhaps the condition is not recognised to the same extent.

These two conditions have concerned the technical aspects of making speech sounds, but there are others which stem from difficulties in understanding the content of any conversation. Let's look briefly at these now.

Semantic and pragmatic disorders

Children with semantic and pragmatic disorders are identified because of their unusual speech characteristics. They may not understand what is being said, or they may use words inappropriately. This means that sustaining interactions with others is hard and so they may have difficulty joining in group activities. This affects their social development and impacts on their self-esteem. Again there are different aspects to consider.

'Semantic' means understanding the meaning of words: such difficulties may also be called 'receptive language disorder'. With this difficulty children fail to understand feeling states such as anguish or jealousy or have difficulty dealing with abstract concepts, i.e. things happening at another time or place. They are much happier depending on concrete artefacts, i.e. things that are present and can be seen and touched.

Pragmatic has a different meaning. 'Pragmatic' means 'knowing what to say when' in a manner appropriate to the context, i.e. adapting conversations depending on the people, their reactions and the places where they are held. Children with these difficulties do not grasp the subtleties within conversations which may come through intonation or sarcasm or the colour which comes through idioms. They know the meaning of the individual words but take them literally – 'get lost' means just that. And of course everyday language is full of such expressions. Imagine Flora's confusion when at parents' night, her teacher explained that 'Flora is out of her seat at the drop of a hat.'

A second difficulty comes in not acknowledging reciprocity in a conversation – children who don't know how to take turns and so dominate the interaction. They also have difficulty in realising the amount of information that is appropriate. And so the questioner asking 'How are you?' and expecting the answer, 'just fine!' is bombarded by lots of detail. And of course people tend to avoid those who say too much. They may also interrupt conversations with apparently unrelated observations with the result that any conversation closes down.

But these children have good vocabularies, they can speak at length and can articulate clearly. However they tend to say more than they understand, they don't allow turn taking; they talk too much and have difficulty understanding non-literal interactions. And so they tend to be avoided, which is not a happy state of affairs at all. They need help to understand the techniques of conversation-making as a first step in their programme of therapy.

Selective mutism

While some children speak too much, others choose not to speak at all and this condition is called selective mutism. These children who may speak quite fluently with good vocabularies at home or where they are secure and comfortable, literally 'freeze' in a new situation and may not utter a word, perhaps for several months. Sally's mum explains her daughter's difficulty.

Sally comes in from nursery, happy as the day is long and she tells me all the things she's done that day. According to her, she has 'played with lots of boys and girls in the house corner and made snack for the others who said how good it was'. I assumed that she was chatting away and was horrified when the teacher explained that Sally came into the nursery every day, immediately grabbed hold of the doll's pram and stood by it at the radiator, neither moving nor speaking, in fact ignoring anyone – teacher or child – who came near. There was no way she could be persuaded to join in.

What was wrong? This kind of reaction can arise from social anxiety – it is a psychological problem where children become unable to speak – they are not just being obstinate. More girls than boys tend to be affected and they are usually of average or above average intelligence, although some may have learning difficulties. The children are likely to have a sensitive, rather vulnerable personality and although programmes of therapy help, progress tends to be slow and in times of stress the difficulty may re-emerge. The most effective intervention is to stay positive and give lots of praise, or non-verbal support if that is more acceptable, so that the children's confidence is boosted and they gradually learn to cope in social situations.

Language difficulties within Down's syndrome

Many children who have Down's syndrome have difficulties with auditory processing, i.e. making sense of the sounds they hear. This may make them reluctant listeners and cause them to be cut off from learning more about speech. Unfortunately, intermittent glue ear, which many of the children have quite regularly, means that hearing is often difficult especially in the winter months when colds may already be causing problems. This is particularly unfortunate if it occurs at a critical learning time, because then auditory difficulties are added to the problems of listening, retaining the information and then decoding it, i.e. making sense of what is heard.

Expressive language may be very slow to develop too and a multisensory approach is likely to be best here. Allowing the children to handle objects so that they can feel their shape and texture is a good idea, for they understand best when they have 'concrete props' like this, rather than being asked to visualise things that are not present or events happening at another time. Feeling movements (e.g. jerky movements) that let them appreciate how a puppet moves instead of showing them a picture or even a real puppet, can help the children internalise the learning and retain the meaning of the words.

In children with Down's syndrome, there may be physical cause for difficult articulation and that is that their palates may be high and arched and their tongues may be large for the space they have. This makes manoeuvring the speech apparatus to form sounds awkward and the resultant speech unclear.

And so language difficulties are complex – as difficult to understand as they can be to treat. However, as language is so pervasive throughout the child's life, early intervention is essential to the quality of that life. Luckily, at least some of the therapy can be disguised as play activities so that children are motivated to practise and hopefully improve so that they can make progress before their self-esteem is too badly affected by not being able to join in. It is vital that these children can make their opinions and feelings known.

Helping children with language difficulties play

Children with speech difficulties are going to be stressed when they have to 'talk out' at length and without preparation. One game which can give them confidence is to have the children in a circle tossing a ball or balloon to one another. The point of this game is that the children have to call out the name of the child who is to receive the ball – just the one word. The child can take time to prepare the word and the throw at the same time and this covers any delay. If children have profound difficulties, then the adult can be beside them in the circle and call out the name at the same time, thus strengthening the sound that is made.

Other games like Chinese whispers can be fun if the child with difficulties starts off the game – no one expects clear enunciation all along the line and so the child with speech difficulties can see that others can make mistakes too and not be distressed.

Attention deficit disorders (ADD and ADHD)

Although the names of these disorders are often used interchangeably, there is a significant difference. Listen to parents talking about their children. First, Helen, Ann's mum. She explains,

The teacher says that Ann could do much better at school but she won't concentrate on her work. Apparently she wanders around the classroom, won't settle and distracts the other children too. She's bright and sometimes I wonder if school is too easy to keep her occupied. I kind of suggested this to her teacher and she immediately got back with, 'Well, she doesn't always get her work correct does she, in fact unless I stand over her she doesn't even finish it.' She was obviously thinking 'Ah, here's another mother who thinks she has a genius' but I wasn't suggesting that. The thing is that she will spend ages drawing and painting at home. She draws lots of detail and can concentrate then. She will listen to stories quite happily when she's tired, although she prefers to be on the go during the day. But it seems that at school she finds it really difficult to pay attention and, according to Ann, the teacher 'is getting cross and shouting a lot', but what can we do?

Darren's story is different. Marie and Jack have just been told that their six-year-old son has ADHD or attention deficit hyperactivity disorder. Listen to their account of their child's difficulties.

Darren will never sit still – never at peace. He's on the go all day long and we are at the stage of begging for someone to do something. He'll run up and down the stairs endlessly, somersault on to beds and climb anything climbable. When the GP said 'What do you need?' I said 'A set of chains for him and a dark room for me because I can't take much more.' As a baby he hardly slept and he's been on the go ever since. The minute he could walk, nowhere was big enough to hold him – he would climb over any barrier and disappear. He got to the bus terminus when he was four and if a friend hadn't spotted him he'd have been off! When I'm at my wits' end I wonder how I would cope if he did disappear and we had to get the police to trace him. No one knows what it's like – endless rows and pleading with him to think of us, how we feel, but Darren just doesn't listen; he pulls away and starts running all over again. He won't listen to reason. I spend a lot of time crying. We must have done something wrong because other children aren't like this. The whole family is distracted and Mum who used to offer to have him for a bit just can't cope any more. What are we going to do?

Neither of these children is making the most of their time at school. Both have difficulty concentrating or paying attention but whereas Ann will sit at things she enjoys, Darren refuses to be interested for more than a minute in anything at all. These two case studies point out the difference between ADD and ADHD and explain why the 'H' stands for hyperactivity.

The characteristics of children with poor attention spans are:

- distractibility
- inability to sit still for long
- constant fidgeting
- impulsivity (acts before thinking)
- won't take turns
- disruptive, annoying others.

These could well describe a child with ADD, however Healy (1996) explains that to be given the diagnosis ADHD accurately, the child must show 'excessive physical activity' which Darren certainly did. Unlike Ann he had no periods of stillness. When Ann was at home following her own agenda she was seen as 'very lively', in other words the parents could cope. Ann had sufficient interests to keep her busy at least for a time, whereas Darren just couldn't settle at all and all the members of the family were suffering by his constant movement.

ADHD is a term every teacher knows. It seems to be given readily, although to be accurate it should only be given in extreme cases where some organic brain dysfunction is suspected. However it is not easy to provide criteria that will show the distinction between normal restlessness and pathology. There are no neurological tests that will prove that the condition exists. To cloud the diagnosis further, it has been found that children given the label ADHD can control themselves in novel, one-to-one situations and if they get frequent rewards – of the kind that they value. This is one behaviour modification strategy which seems to work, but it is not easy to carry it out, especially if there are lots of other children wondering why, when they sit still, they don't have rewards too.

It is essential that these children are helped because:

- 90% are unproductive in schoolwork;
- 90% underachieve in school;
- 20% have reading difficulties;
- 60% have serious handwriting problems;
- only 5% go on to Higher Education (compared to 25% in the general population in the USA).

(Arcelus and Munden 1999)

As many children with ADHD are likely to be intelligent children who are hindered by the core symptoms of the condition, ways to reduce the effect of these must be found. These children along with every other child have the right to a full and profitable education.

Ritalin and medication therapy

Ritalin, properly regulated and administered, is a drug which helps children to settle and focus and there are children and parents who have found that it has made a huge difference to their lives. Why then, do GPs not give it to all children who are restless and disruptive, because then life would be simpler, would it not? The first consideration is that medication does not help all children. Twenty to 30 per cent do not respond although they show no side effects either. The second point is that there can be well-recognised negative effects. Once the drug is stopped the hyperactivity often returns and constant use means that greater doses are needed to have the same effect. An unfortunate side effect of this is that if Ritalin is given in larger doses for longer times, it can actually dull reasoning ability and so the learning it was supposed to promote just doesn't happen (Healy 1996).

There is much media interest in Ritalin and this can distort what actually is happening. If, for example, cases that haven't worked are taken in isolation and the full picture is not given, a distorted picture of the usefulness of the drug results. Sometimes 'outcomes' can focus on difficulties which the children have had for a long time and which are not really related to the condition or the effects of Ritalin or any other medication. Or perhaps the children were given an incorrect dosage or failed to take their medication as advised. The effects of medication need close monitoring and changes in behaviour need to be reported early. To be able to do this, all the adults need to know what the medication is; the pre-existing conditions the child has; the advised dosage and when it should be given and possible side effects to look out for.

No medication cures ADD or ADHD. Its aim is to reduce the primary neurological symptoms so that the child can access learning and socialising in the best possible way.

Attention

In every classroom on every day, someone is sure to be told to pay attention. What is this 'attention' that merits this advice? It is the ability to stay focused on a task and to learn from it; learning being shown in the child knowing something or being able to do something that was not possible before. This requires motivation, or willingness to be engaged, the intellectual competence to make sense of what is to be learned and an absence of factors such as distractibility or poor motor control which comes from conditions like dyspraxia. (Distractibility is caused by a 'fault' in visual perception, which means that the children can't cut out distractors in their environment and they learn best when they are in a quiet, still place.)

Attention, then, is vitally important in that it determines what a child learns. It gives the child control over the time spent on a task and the best chance of benefiting from it.

Different aspects of poor attention

Some children identified as having poor attention can be intellectually very bright, but, being creative thinkers, 'something else out there' pulls them away from the task at hand. They may be the dreamers, perfectly capable of completing work but lacking the motivation to stay on task, or they may be divergent thinkers who visualise a better way to do something . . . and time runs out. For these reasons their written work may not reflect their capability.

Then there are the impulsive children who act before considering the consequences. They begin to paint before considering the scale of what they are trying to portray and land up disappointed with the results. They rush across the road to see a friend without looking; they rip up a piece of work before they have made a good copy. This is a personality trait at the other end of the continuum from 'reflective' children who ponder on the consequences of actions so long that they may never get the task done at all. They could be accused of paying too much attention!

And there are the children who sit quietly enough but without showing any spark of interest. They don't concentrate either – is the work too difficult or not interesting enough? What can be wrong? McGuinness (1985) claims that inattention can be caused by environments that are 'too overwhelming or insufficiently compelling'. She is removing the 'fault' from the child and placing it with those that create the learning environment.

But, unfortunate as it is, there have always been children who are bored, even though work had been planned to match their interests and their capabilities. So why, at this moment in time, should there be such an increase in the number of children who don't pay attention and who can't sit still? Some hearsay accounts may be worth considering.

These children spend much of their lives surrounded by noise. The TV goes on first thing in the morning. They come to school in cars with radios blaring and so they have to shout to make themselves heard. They don't know how to speak quietly. And if there's a teenager at home, the thumping music will be blaring out long past their bedtime. They can't cope unless they are surrounded by noise! It's very worrying.

(Teacher of seven-year-olds)

It's all these e-numbers, and additives in the juice and the food that they eat. When I poured all the bottles of squash down the sink, my children didn't like it, but almost immediately they were calmer. They think they are having these expensive bottles of water – I did buy them one each to get the fancy bottles, but I fill them out of the tap now. I'm now going to find what has been added to that – let's hope there are no chemicals which make it harmful too!

(Mum of four children aged between 3 and 12 years)

Can nutrition affect how children learn?

According to research by Richardson (2000) the answer to this question is 'Yes it can'. This research into fatty acids claims that providing children with a supplement of fatty acids (available from chemists) or increasing their intake of foods which contain fatty acids, for example tuna, will make a significant difference to their restlessness, reduce their clumsiness and increase their ability to cope in a complex learning environment. It is stressed that these nutritional supplements are not drugs, but natural foods that provide 'good things' enabling the children to settle and absorb the learning that is going on around them. Research is continuing and wider trials are being set up to evaluate these claims.

What can be done for those children through play?

As yet there are no clear answers why some children fail to attend. One strategy that has been shown to help is role play, where the child with the difficulty chooses the theme and assigns 'parts' to one or two other children. The adults have to be ready to ask the right kinds of questions, such as how would the characters dress or how would they feel when a development took place, i.e. questions which would extend the thinking and possibly the game without taking the control of the game away from the leading child. If that child abandons the game as well he might, then the adult who is knowledgeable about it can carry on, so that the others aren't disappointed by being left high and dry, for there are no magical instant solutions.

Most often children with ADD or ADHD will join in readily to any play situation – the difficulty comes in keeping their attention, for they often prefer to go off to try something else. Sometimes giving them an important job, such as holding the storybook and turning the pages as the teacher tells the story, works for a time, as does giving them a picture list of things they might do. But it is not easy to keep them on task until they have made some progress. As with all children, finding their interests and building learning/play activities to match is the strategy most likely to work, while the most important thing is to keep them safe.

A last word mentions cultivating a quiet, positive atmosphere and giving lots of praise in the form of rewards. It is essential to discover what kinds of rewards will be acceptable, however, because subtle asides like 'Good lad, that's good work' don't seem to mean enough. The children prefer tangible evidence of their good work. Trying to keep calm and 'catching the children being good or staying on task' is also sound advice. This is a lot easier than it sounds but it is a way in which adults can act as 'constructive, thoughtful coaches for the children' (Healy 1996).

As this section on attention deficit disorders finishes, a final word must concern the classification or labelling of children. There is often unclear knowledge of the etiologies of these conditions and it can be very difficult to produce criteria that are reliable and fair to all the children. The borderlines between those that have a condition and those that are free from it are blurred. Adults have to understand the different conditions and be sympathetic to the difficulties they cause, but concentrate on observing each individual child, because each of them may amaze by the progress they make. Then the children can be proud of what they have achieved. This is most likely to occur if informed adults set realistic and attainable targets, i.e. goals that can be achieved with a reasonable amount of effort. Only in a carefully structured stress-free and positive environment is this likely to happen.

Down's syndrome

Down's syndrome is caused by the presence of an extra chromosome, so that the children have 47 not 46 which is the usual pattern. This means that all of the children will have some degree of learning difficulty, ranging from mild to severe. However, this is not the same as having a global developmental delay, which could be addressed by preparing learning materials suitable for a younger child. Children with Down's syndrome have 'a specific learning profile with characteristic strengths and weaknesses' (Alton 1998) and this affects all aspects of their development. It is vital that professionals appreciate the components of this profile so that they understand how they can differentiate learning activities in ways that encourage the children to develop all the skills that they have. Professionals must remember that children with Down's syndrome vary as widely in their development and the progress they make, as any other group of children who do not have their difficulties. So they must not limit their expectations by some 'typical' picture because this may only represent their child in some superficial way. May's mum explains.

When I told people that May had Down's syndrome, they immediately seemed to know all about it. 'Never mind,' they said, 'they are such happy children and so lovable, they'll give you lots of pleasure.' Another person who came over to the buggy asked, 'Where is the nearest special school?' and one elderly woman even said, 'Ah well, you won't have to worry about jobs . . . '. May was just two at the time and yet people seemed to know how she would cope. They had her future all mapped out. Possibly they were trying to comfort me, but I felt my child had become anonymous and a picture of some other child had taken her place. It was very unnerving . . .

In these first six months or so, I was amazed at May's development, in fact there didn't seem to be too much wrong – she was just a bit floppy and slower to sit up than her brother had been, but she laughed with us and enjoyed all our little games and she's been able to learn lots of things even although she doesn't say a lot. We just recognise achievement in a different way now and we celebrate what she can do (Figure 3.9). We try to encourage her all the way, but of course we worry about her difficulties too. We have to avoid being over protective because she must learn to be independent. The nurse at the clinic explained that it was best to see her as a normal child who has to learn the ways of the world and that too many cuddles could actually hold her back. We have to remember that she's May first, not just a child with Down's syndrome.

As May grew, her parents recognised that her development was slower and that she stayed longer at each stage than her brother had done. The differences became more apparent as she grew, but this was offset to some extent by her personality – her family called her a ray of sunshine who could make them put all their worries into perspective. Moreover, she attended mainstream school and was happy there. Most of the other children were supportive and they learned from May just as she did from them. She had a number of ear and chest infections which hampered her learning, but she made significant progress and her teacher found her 'an asset to her class'.

Figure 3.9 May likes to paint her nails

Let's look then at the sensory perception of Down's children now and find how they take information from their environment to aid their learning; the physical factors which facilitate or impede their learning; and what adults and other children can do to enhance their learning through play.

Sensory perception

Sensory perception includes visual, auditory, tactile, kinesthetic and vestibular input.

Visual perception

Most children with Down's syndrome have strengths in this area. They have a strong visual awareness which means that they learn most readily through seeing. This means that they learn from all the children around them – a terrific bonus, as these children will provide role models of the right age and learning stage which the Down's children can imitate ... provided that the environment is not too busy or confusing. Careful classroom organisation can ensure that the children sit near others who provide good role models, i.e. empathetic children who will not overwhelm the Down's child (again the three Ss, stimulation and support without suffocation, are important words to keep in mind) and whose learning stage is just beyond theirs, so that achieving the same sorts of things seems possible, as does joining together in play. Children with Down's syndrome are often very keen to do as their peers do and when this happens, adults can 'keep back'. If they do this, i.e. observing from a distance and intervening only when really necessary, their presence does not inhibit other children from coming to play and learn with the affected children. This also prevents the children from becoming too dependent on one adult, for they are better to have the wider experience of interacting with more than one person. The distress caused by that one person leaving could also be alleviated if there was another well liked replacement.

As the children learn best visually, lots of brightly coloured visual aids and 'hands-on' resources are needed. These give sensory feedback – pictures and models or solid shapes can be retained and studied again after the learning episode is over. Perhaps the children with Down's syndrome could paste their picture aids into a scrapbook so that they have a diary to help them remember the key points in the lesson. Other children in the class could do this too, so that everyone was involved together. Differentiation could require the more able children to draw the objects rather than paste them, or they could write accompanying stories or poems, or colour a border, whatever would keep them meaningfully occupied and allow the children with Down's a little more time to complete their task. All of these suggestions are to help overcome the poor short-term memory which hampers retention of learning.

Visual impairment

Although children with Down's syndrome learn most easily through their visual sense, many have some problem with their sight, 60 to 70 per cent of them needing glasses before they are seven. This means that learning materials have to be adapted to help the children stay on task, for example through using darker print or having larger pictures which stand out without being confused by too much background detail. Luckily, many storybook pictures can be enlarged on the photocopier so that the children can use their visual sense to the full. Of course the pictures have to be held steadily or be placed well within the children's line of vision.

Auditory perception and impairment

Many children with Down's syndrome find learning by listening difficult, because they experience some hearing loss, especially in the first years which are critically important for learning language. Over 50 per cent of children suffer from glue ear which can recur frequently, especially in the winter when colds and other infections are rife. Often these children have smaller sinuses and ear canals so that infection doesn't drain easily. Sometimes they require hospital treatment causing them to miss school. Some children have a sensorineural loss caused by developmental 'faults' in the ear and the nerves which carry the sounds to the brain. Professionals have to recognise these difficulties and be able to tell when the children aren't hearing properly, for they could well be misled into thinking the children are being inattentive or unmotivated, when in fact instructions have not been heard.

The vestibular sense that contributes to balance is affected by ear infections and as balance is a central factor in being able to move well, the children's movement patterns will be clumsy and uncoordinated when their balance signals coming from the nerves in the ear are miscued. Assistance with balance can come in the form of providing a beanbag at 'sitting on the carpet times' and ensuring that their desks and chairs are the correct size and really steady. Working on large apparatus needs close supervision just as in any other potentially dangerous area.

Children should sit at the front of the class, near the teacher and beside their friends, so that their hearing and other forms of support can be maximised. And as these children are good visually, it is very helpful if the staff can back up their verbal communications with gestures and facial expressions. This will ensure that messages are understood. Teachers can help in other ways too and these will benefit all the children in the class. Perhaps they could repeat another child's correct answer (thus reinforcing the learning) and write just one or two key words on the board (if this is done using simple words, the children have a visual image, i.e. another means of learning in their preferred mode).

Kinesthetic sense

This sense, which relays positional information (i.e. it tells children where they are functioning in the space around them) is sometimes poorly developed. The sense is subdivided into:

- kinesthetic awareness (which tells how near or far away people and things are);
- body awareness (which tells where each body part is in relation to the others); and
- body boundary (which tells where the body ends and the outside world begins).

If one or all of these components are not doing their job properly, the children's movement will be ungainly and imprecise. Spills and tumbles happen often in the day. These can result in lots of scoldings or impatient moves such as pushing the child aside to mop up the juice before it stains, which, if happening constantly, do affect the confidence and the competence of the children who become nervous of trying again.

Responding

Children with Down's syndrome who have problems with their auditory short-term memory, i.e. where understanding and processing spoken language occurs, will find it difficult to remember and respond to verbal instructions. They are likely to need longer to reply and will be glad not to be rushed. This, combined with difficulties in controlling their speech apparatus (some children have tongues which are rather large for the space which holds them, and so manipulating them to form sounds quickly is very difficult), means that conversations can be stilted and not reflect the level of understanding the children possess. These points are important when making assessments about their progress.

Listening and reading

Because the children may not hear sounds clearly and so not match the sound to the symbol which it represents, the phonological path into reading may not be the best choice. The Down's Syndrome Association recommends the whole word approach which allows the children to build up a sight vocabulary and only gradually introducing phonics to decode words when the children are hearing well and when they have the confidence to attempt a second approach. Because the children learn best visually, reading is very often the curriculum area that gives lots of satisfaction and merits positive acclaim. This is very good news, for reading can be used to help understanding in all the curriculum areas; it can extend vocabularies and stimulate imaginations, and perhaps best of all it can help the children to realise that they can do what other children do. They can be part of the crowd, which is what everyone wants.

Social behaviour

Children with Down's syndrome are known as happy children, usually smiling and willing to give lots of hugs. This endears them to lots of people who very often respond in the same way. They love to be with other children and follow and imitate what they do. This gives the other children's self-esteem a boost and so they are usually welcomed into a group. However it has been claimed that these youngsters can use their social wiles to prevent them facing a new learning situation. They work out that a big smile can very often divert the teacher – and so social competence can be counter-productive, in the long run preventing them learning the things they need to know.

But of course, these children aren't happy all of the time. They have to work so hard to try to overcome their difficulties that they get frustrated and upset just like everyone else. However, there are no behaviour difficulties specific to this group of children.

The children with Down's syndrome can lose out in whole-class teaching especially if there is a lengthy explanation requiring a lot of listening at the start as they can be distracted quite easily. They work best in twos or small groups especially if the other children help to keep them focused on the task, perhaps by finding their jotter for them, giving them a quiet reminder of the job to be done or just through providing a role model who is on task.

Physical factors affecting fine and gross movements

Hypotonia (low muscle tone)

Children with Down's syndrome usually have low muscle tone which means that their joints are not firmly fixed in their sockets. This results in movement patterns being floppy and unstable, i.e. clumsy. Their gross motor patterns, such as walking, running or kicking a ball, may all be affected by this lack of strength, which affects coordination as well. Fine motor skills such as writing, drawing, cutting or fastening buttons are awkward too – they are all hampered if the shoulders are not stable and fingers are not strong. Children often adopt a strange pencil grip to compensate; for example to add extra strength they may clutch the pencil and press as hard as they can, breaking the lead and tearing the paper as they do. This is static strength not the dynamic kind required for continuous movement. Cursive writing is easier than print because once the writing action has begun, the momentum can help the fluency of the action (i.e. there is less stopping and starting than is necessary when using print).

How can they be helped through play?

The children's sociability and their willingness to imitate helps them join in lots of play activities, although their 'performance' will be that of a younger child. Play is a happy learning medium, as the children can choose what they wish to do and learn at their own pace. The play corners in the nursery and in the early years' classrooms, (see Appendix 2) are structured to encourage play which relates to the coping competences needed in 'the activities of daily living' and so as they play, the children are building a repertoire of useful skills. Gentle interventions come from adults who can see the most appropriate ways to extend the children's learning without pressure or stress. They will also choose stories or have chats that will reinforce the learning that has occurred, thus helping information to be retained. Many of the activities in Chapter 5, such as 'Simon says', help the important abilities to be developed.

It is worth noting that Hallidie-Smith (1987) reassures parents and professionals that activity is not likely to harm children with a heart defect. The claim is that 'Only very rarely is exercise dangerous ... and if there is severe aortic stenosis, the treatment is surgical relief.' She suggests that children know their own limits and so restrict the level of activity they choose to do. However adults would need to be careful about recognising if this was so and err on the safe side till this was established. It is essential that any orthapaedic problem is very carefully considered before activities such as forward rolls are permitted, for instability at the atlanto-axial joint can lead to dislocation of the neck vertebrae resulting in neurological damage to the spinal cord. Twenty-two per cent of children and adults with Down's syndrome are likely to have this instability, so any exercise that places pressure on the head and neck muscles should be avoided (Tredwell et al. 1990).

Communication between parents, therapists and teachers

Communication between all the groups of professionals is vital if the best strategies for individual children are to be chosen and if the children are not to be confused by conflicting messages. Diaries of progress compiled by the parents and professionals are essential if these children, just like any others, are to reach their full potential. (Communication between parents, therapists and teachers is also discussed in Chapter 4.)

To finish this section on Down's syndrome, let's listen to May's mum again.

We wondered about choosing a special school because the teachers there would have more time to help May. We also wondered if other parents would resent May taking up the teacher's time. After some months a group of parents came up to me and said that they felt that helping May had been excellent for their children. They had learned to be less selfish, they knew that May loved them all and now they loved her too. That was the best day of my life.

And so, when all the children, no matter what their difficulties are, are included as equals in the school community, the learning can surely surpass any that comes out of books.

CHAPTER 4

Communicating, nurturing self-esteem and tackling bullying

Communication among parents, teachers, psychologists and therapists

In an ideal world, the help and support given to all children with special needs would be shared and discussed by all the people who interact with them and the outcomes would be monitored and regularly evaluated. The parents are the children's first educators (Atkins and Bastiani 1988) and as such are the people who provide the home, i.e. the first learning environment, and decide on its scope and its kind. This is critically important, especially if, as Trevarthen (1993) claims, '50 per cent of all learning happens in the first five years'. Parents know the most intimate details about their children, e.g. whether they were easy or difficult to nurture, and about the early achievement of skills, i.e. when the first 'milestones' were achieved (e.g. at what age the children smiled and communicated with their parents; whether they crawled; when they learned to walk and talk). They understand the kinds of things that please the child and those that cause dismay and have the first insights into their preferred mode of learning. They know what sorts of interests the children developed as they grew and the context in which this took place. Only they can provide information regarding any illnesses, injuries or allergies that may have impinged on their children's development in some way, or genetic cues or family traits that could help other professionals have a full picture of their child.

Unfortunately there can be both conceptual and psychological barriers to sharing this information. Some parents may not recognise the importance of the part they have played. They may think it doesn't matter, that it is only the picture 'now' that is relevant. Perhaps some parents hope that school will be a new start and that the professionals there will be able to do things they can't.

Gina explained,

> Thank goodness he's away to school. The teachers will sort him out because I can't. I'm too soft I know, but if I cross him he runs wild and screams, so it's easier to give in and get some peace – he'll have to behave in school, won't he?

Gina realised her son had a behaviour difficulty but some parents are genuinely unaware that their children have difficulties at all. This may be because the children have been sheltered with lots of attention, with everything done for them so that difficulties have not emerged. More commonly, children can react quite differently in the familiar setting of their own home where expectations and reactions are known, than in the much more bewildering business of school. There they have to learn a number of new routines, where to go, what to do, how to interact with lots of adults and other children and cope with lessons as well. No wonder some children become fraught with the enormity of it all.

The early years' school staff are used to observing and evaluating the behaviour of lots of young children of the same age; they know what they should be able to do. They may be the first to become concerned that the child 'avoids social play, does not understand the codes of social conduct in the classroom, has unusual qualities to their conversation and imaginative play, an intense fascination with a particular topic and clumsiness when writing or drawing or playing with a ball' (Attwood 1998). And so the teacher may have to explain to the parents that their child is showing the classic signs of a specific learning difficulty and of course this causes great distress. The parents may well reject the suggestion or ask if it is the school that has caused it and remove the child from the school altogether. Most teachers will look for help from the educational psychologist, even sharing hypothetical observations so that confidentiality is not breached before the parents are informed. They will anticipate a battery of questions from parents who have not been prepared for such tidings, questions such as 'What has caused it?', 'Will he grow out of it?', 'How long will it take?', 'Where do we get help?', 'How soon will help be available?', 'Does medication help?', 'Are there side effects?' and 'How will he cope when he's older?' Teachers have to be ready with at least some of the answers and offer what comfort they can.

Many parents are anxious that their children don't begin school 'with a label which tells teachers they can't do things'.

Tom, Helen's dad, explained that their GP had said to 'be realistic, to lower his sights for Helen', but he was deeply dismayed by this suggestion. That was something he would never do and he was anxious that this philosophy would not drive the practice in Helen's school. Tom was very aware of the effects of the self-fulfilling prophecy, i.e. that teachers might change their approach according to what they were told the child could achieve. He wanted to avoid this possibility. He worried that, 'If the staff think Helen will never be able to do things, they'll maybe accept that and not push her enough. Helen daydreams and could do a lot more if she would only try...' He wanted to be kept informed of what the targets were and when they were achieved.

Others may feel they will be blamed for poor parenting skills.

'What have we done wrong?' asked Alan and Grace. 'We have this lovely boy and yet he just can't do the things other children do. It must be something we've done. Are there special ways to help children that we don't know about? We feel we must have let our son down – where did we go wrong?'

These parents were anxious to share their worries and supposed 'inadequacies' and were ready to follow any advice, but it is not difficult to understand that many parents would be much more reticent in case there were things that they could have done. They may fear that they could be blamed for not knowing about them and trying them out.

Some parents are afraid that teachers won't have the time to speak with them when there are 30 or so other children to be settled and taught. They may be afraid of being seen as pushy or overanxious parents. 'Just getting into school' can be daunting for some if their school experience was in the days when parents were kept firmly at the gate. In those days, education was not seen as the partnership it is claimed to be now.

And what of the teachers themselves? They can feel guilty and inadequate too. Perhaps they haven't heard of the syndrome that the incoming child has, or perhaps, for a host of reasons, they have not had time to read up about it. They may well be concerned that 'reading up' is not enough, but where are newly trained teachers to get the necessary 'hands on' experience?

David, a newly qualified teacher, explained:

> I knew that I was to have two children with quite severe reading difficulties in my class and that was fine, because I had been taught about dyslexia in the university and I read up the latest information about the best ways to help. But there was a breakdown in communication somewhere and when, on the first day a parent told me their child, Gary, had Asperger's syndrome, I was choked. I had heard the name but didn't really know what it was. I was angry not to have had time to prepare. I didn't know whether to be honest and admit it, or try to bluff it out to give myself time, but my face told the parents I had little idea about their child's difficulties and even although I explained I would find out, we were off to a bad start.
>
> When I went to the office, I found that the parents had written in to me personally during the holidays, being unsure where their child was to go to school until then, but their letter had got submerged in a pile of other paper. I phoned them and accepted the blame and thanked them for their helpful communication and reassured them that I would do my best for their son. However, they were still unhappy that a more experienced class teacher wasn't available. The school had to explain that there were children with special needs in all classes and that an experienced support for learning

teacher would be in overall charge of monitoring progress. This helped a bit, but because Gary would need help across the curriculum and especially in social situations, they weren't convinced all would be well. After one or two visits, it turned out that one of their main fears was about bullying in the playground and they were relieved to be told that there were playground supervisors who would look out for all the children and know the ones who were likely to be vulnerable. I also explained the school's policy on bullying and how the school was proud of its ethos, based on positive interventions. But I stayed feeling totally inadequate and so the senior teacher took over the communication with the parents until I got more confident.

Communication difficulties can be compounded when children go out of class for therapy, although again that should be a rich source of discussion between the parents, school professionals, psychologists and therapists, so that every facet of the child's experience is understood. But this takes time and that time is perhaps used up in helping another child. Notes are always passed on – but sometimes the terminology can be baffling to those without specialist knowledge. Lots of therapy can be practised at home and in class the teachers can sometimes incorporate linked activities to help, but sometimes the input is very specialised and non-professionals feel inadequate in carrying it out.

The psychologist may be the first point of contact that the parents or schools have. Psychologists are highly skilled practitioners, experienced in offering advice on how best to proceed and this may mean that they work with the family, just the parents or the child with or without the parents, depending on what is most appropriate. They may use a variety of tests as well as carrying out interviews and collecting evidence of the child's difficulties from teachers and schools to question or to confirm a diagnosis. They do not prescribe any medication but cover issues such as building relationships and explaining social behaviour. Unfortunately there are not enough psychologists to cope with the increasing demand for their skills.

Many schools now have case conferences where adults can come together to discuss the children's progress in all aspects of their lives. This is of especial benefit if the participants can be honest and not be afraid to say that a strategy they tried didn't prove to be helpful for that child on that day. All of the participants have to be convinced that they are all 'on the child's side' and be ready to share the best ways forward. That happens soonest when everyone has the maximum information, because only then can realistic, i.e. challenging, but attainable, targets be set.

Parents, teachers and therapists are all vulnerable. All feel bad if their plan does not achieve the desired effect and may conclude that somehow they have failed the child. They must remember, however, that progress can be erratic and can happen some time after the initial learning input when there has been time for reflection and contemplation.

Only through sustaining communication, difficult as it may be, can the children have the best learning home and school environment where goals and the ways to achieve them are shared. This also lets the children know that the adults are working together and that they can't play one off against the other. Through this communication, the children and all the adults can be confident that their children are having the best possible opportunity to do well.

Nurturing the self-esteem of children with special needs

When children are identified as having a special need, one of the major concerns for all those who are anxious about them is that 'nothing else' will hamper their progress and negatively affect their self-esteem, for this would prevent them reaching their full potential. Many children who lack confidence have a low self-esteem because they have always felt themselves to be different in some negative way and adults fear they may be teased, even bullied, especially if they are sensitive and unsure of how to retaliate. To try to ensure that the children's self-esteem will not suffer, those who look after them need to understand:

- what the self-esteem is;
- the kinds of things which could affect it; and
- if teasing/bullying is going on, strategies to help.

What is the self-esteem?

To understand how self-esteem is formed, one or two terms must be understood. The overarching or global term is the self-concept, which is made up of:

(a) the self-image – this is the picture the child has of him- or herself;
(b) the ideal self – the picture of what the child would like to be.

And so the children's self-image is what they see themselves to be, and their ideal self is what they would like to be. The self-esteem depends on the self-perceived distance between the two (Figure 4.1).

The self-esteem is the picture children build of themselves through evaluating the reactions of others. It is sometimes called a tri-dimensional image, in other words the picture is formed by a complex triad of judgements, sometimes explained as 'What I think of myself depends on what I think you think of me.' Cooley (1962) called this the looking glass self. He visualised a person looking in a mirror with another person's reflection behind signalling evaluative cues.

This is quite a difficult concept to grasp, made even more complex because the effect of that other person's evaluations will depend on how his or her opinion is valued. This is why the most influential effect is caused by those who are 'significant others' in the children's environment. In the earliest years these are likely to be the child's parents, but when nursery and school days arrive, the adults

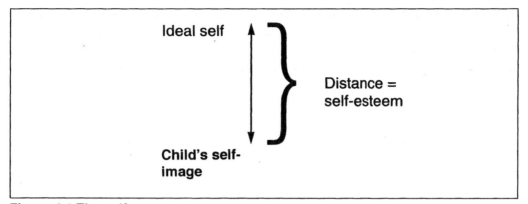

Figure 4.1 The self-esteem

there usually become the ones who are revered. Parents will remember the day when their child countered their own opinions, 'That's not what Mrs so and so (the teacher) said or did' and there's no doubt who, in the child's opinion, was right! Later still the peer group, the children's friends or contemporaries, are the ones who support or destroy this picture and their evaluations can counteract any effort adults make to say their judgements are not true. Hence the children's need to be the same, in case any clothing, hairstyle or way of behaving makes them stand out as being different.

This shifting of 'significant others' tells us that young children's value judgements about themselves are not firmly fixed, although later they become harder, almost impossible in some cases, to shift. Self-esteem is something they learn (Gurney 1987). This means that the early years can be the critical time for giving lots of positive input, for then parents and teachers are still the most influential ones and this gives them the opportunity to show children how important they are. The idea is to have the children's self-evaluations high before anyone can damage them. At least then they have a sound base from which to deflect any hurts.

Two other variables are important. These are the personality characteristics or traits of vulnerability and resilience and they form the polar ends of a continuum. Where the children are placed on this line will determine whether and to what extent they are affected by the judgements of others: the more resilient children being able to shrug off comments which could distress the more vulnerable ones. Many children with special needs come into the vulnerable category, some becoming depressed, even suicidal by the aggressive, hurtful input from other children and some parents too. But some children can have severe disabilities and still have the strength of personality to cope. Both genetic and environmental factors must be very positive and supportive for this to happen.

It has to be said, however, that children with special needs can cause hurt as well – they can retaliate either through frustration at not being able to cope or join in, or because they genuinely do not realise the effect their words or their actions have. One child with Asperger's syndrome laughed out loud as another child was telling of the death of her hamster and of course this was met by disbelief and mutterings. The child had only heard that the hamster was put in a box and thought this was some kind of game. She had had no notion that dying (whatever that might be) was involved. The owner of the hamster could not understand this totally inappropriate behaviour, while the child with Asperger's was baffled by the reaction her behaviour produced. The parents, not appreciating the difficulties of the child with Asperger's, were angry and confrontational till the school took steps to explain. The stigma took a long time to go away however, especially as some of the other children kept the story alive.

Children who have poor motor control can inadvertently cause hurt when they go too fast, can't stop and end up pushing others over. If this happens regularly, other children get annoyed, even begin to retaliate by hitting out and this starts a row and cries of 'It wasn't me!' Resilience and vulnerability play their parts here too. Resilient children will soon forget and become involved in the next activity. They tend to remember the good things in the day and cheerfully take the rough with the smooth, whereas vulnerable children are more likely to dwell on real or imagined hurts and become morose and resentful. This is why two children can 'honestly' give opposite accounts of the same incident. Each has their own perspective of events, which in their eyes are true. In trying to resolve differences, adults need to try to see things from each child's perspective and understand their source – not an easy thing to do.

How children's self-images are formed and how to keep them positive

Harter (1990) claims that it is incorrect to talk of preschool children having a high or a low self-esteem because they make their judgements on a range of separate skills. So they may say 'I can jump and skip' (for very often they talk of their movement skill as being the most important) but they would not consider themselves globally in the sense of 'I am a worthwhile person.' Young children tend to concentrate on evaluating their own abilities; certainly not many preschoolers are heard decrying their friends. Perhaps this is because they are still engaging in solitary or parallel play and this egocentricity prevents them making comparisons as to how well things are being done. When they do talk about their friends, they tend to use surface descriptors, i.e. they will talk about their friend's hair or new dress but usually just stating facts, not with envy. But by age six or seven, the children's experiences have broadened and they have listened to adults who sometimes say things like 'Isn't she shy?' or 'Another girl! Ah well, never mind', without realising that these judgements are being stored away to form part of the child's global self-esteem. It's so easy to speak like this without thinking, and once the words are out they can't be retrieved. I remember saying to a seven-year-old grandchild who had new shoes, 'My goodness Rob, what size are these shoes?', implying of course that they were very big. After some time looking down, he solemnly replied, 'They're the same size as my feet of course!' The moment passed, but a more vulnerable child could have pondered and been upset. This is very important, because a child's self-esteem can affect their willingness to participate in new activities, their concentration, even their motivation to learn at all.

As children grow, more and more outside influences impinge on their self-esteem. The effect of the media displaying the tall, slim, 'cool' child without a blemish (look at the unreal youngsters in Ramsay St.) is enough to make anyone despair!

Establishing a positive ethos

How can adults try to make sure that each child has a positive self-esteem? Certainly the children can't be allowed to feel they have disappointed in any personal way. This doesn't mean they have always to be told they are good, but using positive strategies which 'catch them being good' and offer immediate praise or rewards is a way that works. When instances of unacceptable behaviour do occur, adults must take time to ensure the children know that it was these particular episodes that were disappointing rather than any personal attribute of the children themselves. 'That is lovely work' when the child knows full well it's not helps no one, while 'I know that if you take more time, your cutting out could be neater, and then it would be really good' just might. Pope (1988), a head teacher of children with special needs, explains that 'Telling a child he is good at something when he knows full well he's not, far from raising his self-esteem only reduces it.' In addition she goes on to explain that 'I have been amazed how well children respond to an acceptance of their difficulties when this is coupled with positive activities that can lead to improvements.' And so although tasks may have to be scaled down to provide small measures of achievement, they are none the less important indicators of progress and must be valued as such.

What other strategies might be tried?

If individual children are seen to have low self-esteem, a one-to-one activity where the adult scribes lists of 'things I am good at' for the children, often breaks down barriers and helps their confidence. The children can then colour in the border to make a picture, to go on the bedroom wall perhaps, so providing a positive reminder and hopefully continuing to boost their confidence.

Example

Peter, age five, compiled this list. Marion, his classroom assistant did the scribing.

Figure 4.2 Adam

I am good at getting up early.
I am good at finishing my toast.
I am good at finding the car keys for Mummy.
I am good at keeping clean.
I am sometimes good at sums.
I am good at helping Mrs Jack.

At first Peter couldn't think of anything he was good at, but he became more confident once he saw that small items were important – he didn't have to compare his performance to other people's and be found wanting. Once the game was underway and he felt secure, he was able to share things he wanted to improve and these provided targets for action for a time. This went awry however, when Peter admitted 'I'm not much use at football.' When he was asked if he would like to go and practise however, he was horrified. 'Oh no, I don't want to be good at that!' This caused a blip because Peter began to work out the consequences of his answers. This shows how activities can begin well – Peter had one nice completed picture which had earned him praise and given him, his teachers and his parents pleasure – but when the activity became more complicated, it started to go wrong. The idea had been to practise football so that Peter could join in playground games, but this was not a meaningful reward for him and he was having none of it. Not all efforts are totally successful.

What about children with Asperger's syndrome?

Children with Asperger's are likely to be able to build their self-image. They will be able to tell what age they are, their name, whether they have a sister or brother and the kinds of things they are good at. But because they find it difficult to read other people's reactions to them through interpreting non-verbal cues and facial expressions, it may not be easy for them to form a stable self-esteem. This may be why these children need lots of positive input to reassure them they are doing well; they may need concrete evidence in the form of rewards, such as stickers or other 'prizes' of some sort, because they endure. Transitory verbal praise, which is abstract, may not be enough as it disappears and the child may soon wonder if it ever happened at all.

One innovation that has proved successful was conceptualised by Gurney (1987). He advised:

- teachers praise yourselves;
- teach the children to praise each other;
- teach the children to praise themselves.

How could teachers do this? At the end of the day or at breaks for the younger ones, they could recap on the day's achievements, for example by saying 'Haven't we done well today? We have learned...' – maybe just recapping on three points. Some teachers who tried this, said it made them realise just how much they had achieved. These achievements didn't always or even primarily cover intellectual things. Examples could be 'We all walked down to the hall quietly so the other children weren't disturbed', or 'Today we have started our collage for the Christmas decorations and everyone has worked hard with no squabbling', or 'Today, everyone was kind to one another... everyone was allowed to play, well done!' In this way, special things, which were important to each group of children, could be emphasised, thus reinforcing the learning that had gone on. This could be developed to fulfil the next piece of advice, 'Teach the children to praise each other', by simply adding the rejoinder 'Who did this really well today?' and of course the question could concern the things the children with special needs did, so that they were sure to be nominated by their peers. Having them praise themselves could be tricky if this was to be done publicly, but quiet asides such as 'Tell me the new things you did today' might suffice, especially if the adult could say 'Did you manage to do some of them well? Yes? Good for you!' The approach would depend on the individual child. Some would be reluctant to be noticed while others would have plenty to say.

And of course these subtle interactions could very often remind the children about their playground behaviour – a strategy which could help to overcome bullying.

Bullying

Everyone knows what bullying is, but they may not be aware of its dire and often long lasting consequences. In their *Anti-bullying: Guidelines and procedures for young people* (2000), East Lothian Council in Scotland offer one description. They claim that,

> Bullying in all its forms has a detrimental effect on a person's self-esteem which may lead to feelings related to lack of self-worth, low self-image or self-confidence. It is also likely to happen to people who have low self-esteem... everyone has the right to be listened to and taken seriously. It is everyone's responsibility to make sure this happens.

Most regions have policy documents on bullying and these set out the rights of the children and their parents to have a bully-free time at school and outline the correct procedures to be followed in reporting bullying and acting on the information given. Schools have their own ways of putting these policies into action. These vary from region to region, but the underlying ethos is the same, i.e. that children should be aware that there are different forms of bullying, that those who look on and take no steps to intervene (by for example telling an adult) are guilty by omission and that action will be taken to investigate and resolve the incident.

Different types of bullying

What then are the different types of bullying which young children employ? It is important that the children realise that all of these are bullying strategies and will be treated as such, even if the perpetrators claim they were 'just larking around'.

Physical bullying

This varies from intentionally nudging and pushing to causing physical harm which may need hospital treatment. While the first may not seem as serious as the second, it is likely to be more covert. It destroys confidence through regularity and the bullied child never being quite sure when it is going to happen. Physical bullying also covers incidents that damage property and the children's work. These can be very distressing, especially for children with special needs who may have made a special effort to have lovely work to take home, or for children from less advantaged homes who understand the difficulties in replacing items of clothing or school equipment.

Verbal bullying

Teasing and taunting, name calling and sarcasm all come into this category of abuse. The subject may be to do with ability, age, gender, race, lifestyle (including clothes, hairstyles) or personal features related to size or shape. Some playgrounds will use them all.

Non-verbal bullying

This is often difficult to pin down, especially if the victim doesn't wish to show the gestures or the 'making faces' which caused such hurt. Extortion can range from stealing crisps to personal belongings, to blackmail – the latter usually accompanied by threats of what will happen if the victim 'tells'.

Types of bullies

There are various types of bullies. There are the ones who do the deeds and these may be different from the ones who thought up the actions in the first place and then there are the supporters who encourage them or find subtle ways to keep the incident alive. The incidents themselves may be single or ongoing. Action has to be taken to try to stop them all.

It is difficult to categorise all types of behaviour that cause hurt. Are children who won't let others play, bullies? This may be seen as trivial, but to the isolated child it is the source of tremendous anxiety. Many are able to cope in the classroom but the playground is another whole experience.

What are schools doing to help?

Today, most classes will help children to realise the effects of their actions through planned curriculum interventions, i.e. as an important part of personal, social and moral education. These would include:

- discussions about 'how would you feel if...' concerning various, events and outcomes; and
- role-play situations where the children could act out scenes where emotions run high.

These give opportunities to examine bullying without blame. Hypothetical, but real life situations are set up which discuss or enact the feelings of both the bully and the victim.

In this setting, children get to grips with questions like 'What caused the bully to do these hurtful things?' or 'How does the victim feel?' or 'What should the bullied child do?' These are all put in place so that no child can avert the charge of knowing about bullying and acting in a way that was unacceptable. The vulnerable children are also reassured that bullying is not new, it happens to others too, and most importantly, that if they confide in an adult, they will be believed and help is always at hand.

Strategies in place in many schools now are:

- *an anti-bullying week.* Some schools have a specific anti-bullying week when every class examines that theme. All the classroom discussions, many of the written tasks, the art work and the drama is based on making children aware of how some suffer at the hands of bullies and providing measures to help. These are all age related, with the children themselves suggesting 'rules' for confronting the problem. In this way, the feeling of giving responsibility to the children (just as in play) is maintained.
- *a buddy system where an older child looks out for a younger one.* Careful selection of the pairs can ensure that the vulnerable ones, including children with special needs, are paired with an especially responsible child. This is often helpful as some children will feel more comfortable confiding in another child rather than an adult.
- *allowing vulnerable children to come straight into school rather than spending time in the playground.* Indeed some schools have made this a choice for everyone – to prevent any stigma being attached to those who can't face the playground. This does require indoor supervision and preparation of enjoyable (play?) things for the children to do, but when vulnerable children are relieved of their worries, perhaps coming to school without being upset, professionals have judged the move to be well worth the effort involved. Very often the older responsible children can help the supervisors and so they benefit from having extra responsibility too.

Involving all the adults in the school can help eradicate bullying by the kind of behaviour they demonstrate to their pupils and their colleagues. As a role model they have to be calm and predictable, giving each child the same amount and quality of attention, allocating 'jobs' fairly and 'penalties' too, for very often the children who can't do their sums can check the points system of rewards without any trouble at all and woe betide any teacher who gets it wrong.

Despite everyone's best efforts, in some schools bullying persists. There are so many ways to do it and corners in which to hide, that it is difficult to be sure that it is eradicated and, with a shifting population, that it will stay that way.

CHAPTER 5

More ideas to help children with special needs through play

This chapter provides a selection of ideas to help children play. These are suitable for the range of difficulties children with different special needs show. There are pointers to help extend the children's learning and, accompanying some activities, guidelines to keep the children safe. Because of the overlap of symptoms within the different conditions, a number of play activities can help lots of children and even if these have no specific input for a certain difficulty, they are all there to be enjoyed – they will all help socially and give the children confidence through having participated. No child is going to be harmed by taking part. Some ideas will suit some children more than others and some will need to be altered to make them suitable, but I hope that most of them can be taken forward to provide both enjoyment and help for these special children. Some of the activities may seem very basic, but for children who perhaps don't recognise facial expressions or who can't tolerate much change in their daily routine, they may hold challenge enough. Children with global developmental delay will cope at the level expected of a younger child, so norms linked to chronological age do not always provide realistic expectations. Some of the ideas, or similar ones will possibly be part of the nursery or early years' classroom already, but the analysis of the demands they make on children with special needs and the benefit these children will gain from them is new.

It goes without saying that staff have to remember that some children may be impulsive and not anticipate the outcome of their actions, so safety is of paramount importance. All the usual nursery concerns have to be in place to ensure that the children who have poor balance and/or little sense of self-preservation don't get hurt. So for example there should be lots of crash mats under climbing activities, gates should be securely locked and there should be no running games near sharp corners. No matter what the activity is, it is a good idea to imagine what the most impulsive children would try to do and make sure they could do it safely.

Simple 'follow my leader' games

In small groups, children enjoy marching round a room or in and out of skittles following a leader. The leader can choose the action – skipping, jogging or walking with arms swinging.

When the leader changes, and this is best done often and as the children move, 'Leader changing to James now, everyone else in behind!', the leader often chooses to keep marching. This is the action that seems to give most enjoyment. Children who need hard feedback from the environment through the proprioceptors in their feet to help their spatial awareness are free to thump, while those who have greater tactile sensitivity can do the action lightly, so no one should be upset. The children just love being the leader and quick changeovers mean that everyone can have a turn. In this activity the children are learning about keeping in a line (helping spatial awareness), which they are required to do in school. This also means that they learn to tolerate being near another person and possibly being touched – hopefully the game will provide a means of developing spatial tolerance for the children who find this difficult. Enlarging the possible route, such as giving the children the opportunity to march out of one door and back through another, can be one way of subtly enlarging the space/changing the routine of children who find this difficult.

Once the children have practised lots of actions in a line, they may be ready to show the moves different animals or characters make, such as the clown in baggy trousers, the wooden puppet or a rag doll, and they can try these ideas out all together or singly as the watching children sit in a circle. Sometimes a jingle can help. 'Watch me, I can show!' was written for this kind of activity.

Watch me, I can show!

A tiny rabbit scampers past,
How does he go?
His bobtail popping up and down,
Watch me, I can show!

A great long snake, he slithers past,
How does he go?
He slides around, close to the ground,
Watch me, I can show!

A buzzy bee, he zooms around,
How does he go?
Here and there and everywhere,
Watch me, I can show!

A kangaroo takes great long leaps,
How does he go?
He bounds around, far from the ground,
Watch me, I can show!

A tiny mouse is very quiet,
How does he go?
He peeps right out, then darts about,
Watch me, I can show!

A butterfly floats gently past,
How does he go?
He swoops and lands so daintily,
Watch me, I can show!

A little child can run so fast,
Till (she/he) is all aglow,
Who is that person running there?
It's (child's name),
Don't you know?

C. M.

Circle activities

Sitting or standing in a circle (a safe enclosing space), helps children to be aware of others sitting at their side. Some children find this extremely difficult, because laterality or awareness of 'sidedness' can be slow to develop and not be fully operational till the children are nine or so. Activities like passing a beanbag round or a stick with Blu-tack or coloured tape firmly fixed to each end, soon show where difficulties lie.

Let's analyse what is involved in this circle activity, i.e. in what would seem to be an easy thing to do. First of all the children have to stand still, keeping their place in the ring (not as easy as it sounds for those who have difficulty maintaining their balance in stillness – some children need constant feedback which they get from movement to give them spatial cues). Then they have to balance as they stretch one arm out to the side – and this may not be their preferred hand so clasping may be awkward. The children then have to pass the beanbag or the stick from one hand to the other at the midline of their body. This can be difficult because midline actions may cause confusion. However once the pattern of change has been established, the children should be encouraged to stretch right out in front of them to pass the stick so that they can see the action. This encourages them to take time to make the change and also lets them feel the balance demands of the action, either in holding their body still or in helping them to transfer their weight from one foot to the other. Once the pattern is established they may like to pass the beanbag or stick behind their backs.

'Simon says' and similar games

In the game 'Simon says' the 'leader', out in front and facing a group, gives instructions to them, such as 'Simon says, put your hands on your head.' The fun comes when the instructions are not preceded by 'Simon says', because then the group are to hold still and not obey at all. The speed of the game can be altered to allow children with perceptual difficulties to join in.

These games are always well liked and they are excellent for helping children with poor body awareness feel where their different body parts are and where these parts end and the outside world begins, i.e. they develop their sense of body boundary too. This is important in developing deft movements, such as placing a cup on a table without hitting the edge or spilling its contents.

Understanding emotions

Lots of enjoyable input can be derived from activities which help children to interpret facial expression and body postures. These are important skills as only 10 per cent of the meaning of a conversation is in the actual words – even counting the difference that intonation makes. This fundamental skill proves to be very, very difficult for some children.

The adult asks 'How do you feel today?' or if this is too personal, 'How does Mr Bloggs (or any other toy, preferably one with a large face) feel today?' and the child has to reply with a word describing an emotion (e.g. grumpy, sad, happy, frightened, angry, tired, shivery, bored, hurt, anxious, cross, sorry, lonely, sunny etc.). The child then points to a circle (Figure 5.1) to answer the question 'Which face looks like that?'

The children soon realise that they don't necessarily have to say how they are feeling – it's just a game – but some children will prefer to be totally honest. Substituting a toy can help these children talk about a greater range of emotions.

A development of this game is staff keeping the conversation alive by asking 'What can we do to make (you or the toy) happy?' and 'How will (you or the toy) look then?' The child should point to the circle to show whether the link between feelings and visual expressions is appreciated.

One interaction that used a similar strategy happened in an Edinburgh nursery and has always stayed in my mind as an example of wonderful practice.

Example

It was Ian's first day at school and he was not happy. In fact he sat hard against the wall howling, and when the other children moved in to try to comfort him they were met by roars of rage and violent kicking. The teacher, Carol, sat down a little distance away from Ian but avoided any contact. She picked a furry bear

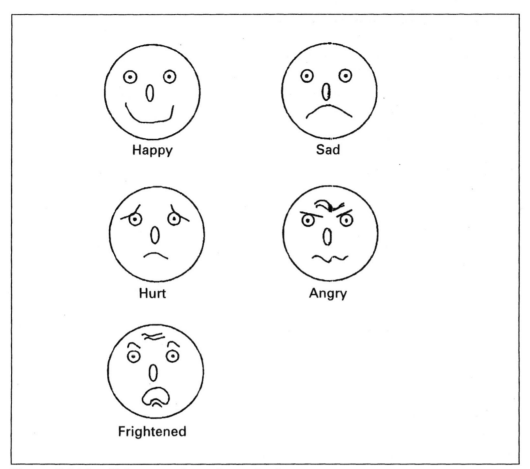

Figure 5.1 Identifying emotions through play

from the toy box and began to stroke it, murmuring soothing words as she did. All her attention appeared to be on the toy but the hidden message was that she was the kind of person who realised how upsetting coming to school could be. Ian gradually began to be interested in what she was doing and his howling changed to sobbing. When he had calmed down a little and could hear, Carol asked 'Could you help me please? This little bear is frightened and upset, he would like you to stroke him too.'

All this time, Carol deliberately avoided trying to hold eye contact with Ian – all her attention appeared to be on comforting the bear. This was much less threatening for the child. As he gradually approached, to see what she was doing, Carol, without speaking offered the toy to the child. He took it, went back to his original place and sat stroking the toy, but as he did he began to look out into the room. His guard was down and he was beginning to want to play. The toy, which had given him a responsible job to do, became his favourite friend until he made friends with other children.

In this instance, the teacher capitalised on the child's natural capacity for caring. By not talking directly to the child she was putting no pressure on him. Yet, by gently stroking the bear, she was demonstrating that she was a caring person. Later, when talking to the child was easier, she complimented him on how well he had looked after the bear. She also made sure the other children knew how pleased she was and this counteracted the rather unfortunate start the child had had.

Thomas the Tank Engine

This series of stories and videos is excellent because the different emotions are displayed clearly on each of the train's faces and their actions match the emotions they portray, for example the sad train chugs slowly and the steam comes out in dark grey puffs. The emotions don't change quickly and so the children have time to see how each emotion is portrayed. They are also depersonalised – the child hasn't made Thomas happy or sad. Lots of discussion about why the train felt sad or happy can follow and some children might volunteer or be encouraged to share experiences from their own lives.

> 'I feel happy when . . .'
> 'I feel sad when . . .'

These observations can form lists to help the staff understand the children's likes and dislikes, their preferences and things to be avoided at all costs. Parents enjoy seeing lists like these because they show the amount of attention their children are receiving. They can also provide lots of surprises. One child claimed that he loved porridge although the nursery never had it and he couldn't be persuaded to taste it at home!

An explanation like 'I feel sad when Darren tells me I'm fat' can also help children realise that their actions can have an effect on how other people feel. Although this will be obvious to some children, the idea will not have occurred to others. Follow-on comments such as 'Oh dear, Darren has forgotten to be kind today; what can we do to make (child's name) happy?' can turn a negative comment into a positive action if the conclusion is something that can be followed through. The response might be 'We'll make a surprise' – it might be baking a cake for that person, making a card, tying up a parcel or doing a drawing. (All of these are good for fine motor skills.) This would be a child-led suggestion, which can be a 'legitimate' part of the curriculum, linking closely to criteria for achievement such as 'finding a practical solution to a problem'. The important thing is that the children are able to follow through the effect of their interpreting an emotional state in someone else, making a positive contribution for that person and then, through answering questions such as 'How do you think (child's name) will feel now?', anticipating the change of emotions and the other non-verbal changes that the surprise will bring.

Sequencing: understanding the order of events

This kind of activity also helps sequencing because it involves planning a series of actions and organising resources to fulfil the plan. This is vital experience for children who have poor organisational and planning skills. It also helps the children cope with activities of daily living and this, in some small way at this stage, contributes to making them more independent people who can choose what they wish to do.

At a basic level some children need help in understanding the order of things they have to do. Staff can ask 'What would you like to do today?' and then help the children think through the preparation, planning and ordering of resources. This can be achieved by asking perhaps 'What do we need to do first?' rather than assuming the planning is understood and doing most of it for the children, just to get the activity underway.

From the moment they get up, some children may need charts, for example to show them the order of putting their clothes on. These children can have the movement abilities to get dressed but not the sequencing skills to know what goes on first. At school colourful timetables can help, often numbered 1, 2, 3, but in the early years this does take away from them having free choice to follow their own interests. However the timetable helps those that prefer the security of an established routine and it may help them avoid 'mistakes' which the other children may point out.

Elise, who had a poor short-term memory, explained,

> When I'm at school everything is very busy and sometimes I can't remember if I've had snack. Sometimes I forget to go the bathroom too and the chart just reminds me, so I don't have to worry about that any more.

The idea of a timetable can be developed into keeping a diary. As lots of children find it difficult to express how they feel, a number of simply drawn expressions on circles and photocopied on to sticky labels can make 'peelable' diary entries. Sometimes children do not realise that adults in school want them to feel good and that they are there to help with emotions just as much as sums. Activities like discussing entries in diaries can help the children appreciate this. Chats with every child, but perhaps longer times with children who need to talk about what caused them to 'have two sad faces in one morning', can be very helpful because these children may not have the language or the confidence to approach and explain. This 'other' method of recording their emotions gives them time to think and the staff a means of starting a conversation.

Understanding emotions in a poem or story

Children enjoy poems and stories and often they are asked to remember the characters and the order of events. As the story unfolds, they may be asked to anticipate the kinds of things that might happen. But less attention is usually paid to the feelings of the characters in the story, for example 'How did baby bear feel when he saw that someone had eaten his porridge?' . . . 'How did he feel when he saw Goldilocks in his bed?'

For example look for the puppet's feelings in this jingle. The children are in twos – Peter the puppet and Jane the puppeteer.

Peter the puppet

I'm Peter the puppet,
Can you see my strings?
My arms are all floppy,
Watch how they swing.

I'm ready to dance now,
Jane, pull my strings tight,
And I'll stretch to the ceiling
With all of my might.

Let me dance now, let me dance now,
I just love to be free.
I can skip round the room now,
Why don't you dance with me?

I go forwards and backwards
And round in a ring,
Dancing's the best way,
The very best thing!

But Jane's got to go now,
Oh, isn't it sad?
She's letting me flop down,
I really feel bad.

For I wanted to keep dancing
All over the room,
Jane, be my best friend,
Come back to me soon!

C. M.

At the start the puppet is a bit sad, longing to be free of his strings that make him feel cramped and rather miserable. Then, when he hears Jane coming he is hopeful and happy, and his dancing and skipping makes him full of joy, energetic, bright, cheery, merry or pleased. When he has done some dancing and Jane has to go, he is annoyed, angry or frustrated but because Jane is his friend, he is hopeful, trusting that she will come back soon. The children can demonstrate these feelings through their movement and children who have difficulties recognising emotions have opportunities to watch the other children and learn from them. They can also try out what to be 'floppy' and 'fully stretched' feels like and practise their skipping. There's a lot of learning potential if jingles like this are analysed in terms of movement possibilities.

Helping children to concentrate

The first thing is to check the children's environment, i.e. where they are to do their work. Their space needs to be quiet, away from passing sounds or windows which offer distraction (blowing leaves on the trees) or temptation (to see what is going on). Children who can't settle, who are constantly finding ways to avoid sitting still, need help and this depends on the degree of distractibility and its source, i.e. whether it is visual or auditory. Having a quiet spot with a chair that doesn't rock and a desk at the correct height to help balance/stability may be enough for some children. Large egg timers can give a visual picture of how long the child should try to stay in place and this can help children understand the passing of time, although watching the sand trickling through can be more entertaining than doing the set task. The nature of the task is the key – if learning activities can be derived from the children's interests, they are more likely to be absorbed. This takes a great deal of time and effort. Simple mapping could be understood through looking at bus routes (children with Asperger's syndrome often have interests like this), just as counting the number of buses going each way could lead to bar charts and simple problem-solving exercises. An example could be if the fare was printed alongside the bus route, in 1ps or 2ps, then the children could work out how to go to the sea or whatever was featuring on the route map, when they should travel and how much it would cost. Classroom assistants are wonderful at helping to make resources like this, and it is a good idea to laminate them so that they can be used for different purposes or different children at different times. Extra preparation has to pay off in the end.

Activities to help development of ball skills

The main ball skills are:

- rolling and retrieving;
- throwing and catching;
- kicking;
- aiming.

Many children have motor learning difficulties which means they do not have the hand–eye or foot–eye coordination or the balance to be able to be proficient in ball skills and yet most children yearn to be able to do them. Analysing the sequence shows how complex these are and shows why children should practise basic actions before adding environmental hazards, for example learning to kick a stationary ball into a goal mouth before attempting to kick a moving one past a goalkeeper.

Releasing a ball at the right time is an essential component (a timing skill), as is being able to move to catch the ball (a tracking skill). One way to help develop ball skills is to follow the steps and stages outlined below.

1. *Tunnels*

In twos facing one another, sitting legs outstretched and apart. Roll the ball into the gap made by the other person's legs. This helps directionality and tracking skills and it's fun when the speed is varied. The good thing is that no time is lost chasing the ball to bring it back. It is firmly held in the tunnel.

This can be developed by the twos joining up into groups to sit in a circle, in the same position (i.e. legs outstretched and apart). The child with the ball chooses where to roll it and the receiver rolls the ball on into the next tunnel. Once the idea is understood, using two balls can give lots of laughs and surprises. Children have to keep alert in case they are the one to receive the ball.

In these sitting activities, balance difficulties are removed. Releasing the ball and tracking its path are good practices and the uncertainty caused by not knowing where the ball is going to go, keeps attention focused in the more difficult second activity.

2. *Rolling and retrieving*

From standing, each child with a ball rolls it ahead and retrieves it before it reaches a line on the floor.

Progress to rolling the ball against an upturned bench and retrieving it on the rebound. This helps judging speed, i.e. estimating the rebound in line with the ability to catch.

Both these practices help timing of releasing the ball and making judgements about how much speed and strength to use. The children see the effect of their actions. They also require the children to make a basket with their hands and to move in line with the oncoming ball to catch it. The children are still in total control, not depending on a partner to roll sympathetically.

3. *Throwing and catching sympathetically with a partner*
The children will need to be helped with the distance between the partners and be shown the stance (opposing foot forward) that allows the long, smooth arm movement of the underarm throw. Although this sounds easy, children with poor three-dimensional vision will turn away rather than catch because seeing the approaching ball late means that they do not have time to make adjustments. If this happens allow them to use a foam ball. It travels more slowly and doesn't hurt if it bumps!

The children can set up mini competitions where they try to beat their own record, such as aiming for five throws without dropping the ball.

4. *Skittle alley*
Rolling the ball to knock down skittles helps in developing a good aim – this can be called ten pin bowling if 'alleys' are constructed. Younger children can make and decorate their skittles, which will topple more easily than the gym ones which are harder to knock over.

Use a variety of balls as skill improves. Foam balls travel more slowly and are easily retrieved, but they don't have much 'go'. Volleyballs are best because they are the 'real thing' but are light enough not to hurt. This activity is good for organisation and planning – also for waiting to take turns and letting one or two others finish their turn before the skittles can be set up again.

Mini practices, which can suffice when children are waiting for their turn on the 'real' skittle alley, can be simply constructed, for example rolling a tennis ball into an upturned bucket. This helps aiming skills, tracking and also with establishing the stance which is the same for rolling and throwing.

5. *Kicking*
Most children love to kick a ball and will happily practise. However, what the inexpert kicker does is to run at the ball and use the point of the foot to send it off in any direction at any speed. To gain control, the children need to stand by the ball and push it just a short distance into a net (to keep the game real), using the inside of their preferred foot. This helps the direction of the kick to be more accurate and the ball goes into the net. Success! This also helps the children to judge the strength that is needed. Pushing the ball into an empty net (a closed skill) needs to be practised before a goalie is added because then two things, i.e. the ball and the position of the opponent, have to be considered. Finally the children can run to kick a stationary ball before getting to grips with a moving ball (an open skill). The terrain (i.e. whether it is rough or smooth) can affect the success and so this has to be part of the learning curve too.

Dribbling the ball round skittles is another form of kicking and in this activity control and judging speed and distance are equally important. The distance between skittles will determine the number of changes of direction and the angle of change which is required, so the arrangement can be adjusted to suit the children's skill. Teachers should remember that in 'races', popular as they are, the skill is likely to disappear as the children become involved with the hustle and bustle of getting to the end and winning. It is better to emphasise control rather than speed.

Using music and rhythm

Music and rhythm can be used in many guises to stimulate or soothe. The Mozart effect (playing classical music to calm children and aid their concentration) is being tried out in schools now to try to calm pupils and keep them on task. Attwood (1998) explains that 'music with a clear and consistent rhythm as occurs in Baroque and Country and Western music' has proved the most helpful.

Example 1 Using music

Sarah has a class of six-year-olds with some children who arrive excited and 'ready to fight with their shadow'. She tried to burn up the tension with an activity programme of stretching and swinging arms first thing in the morning but found that raised the tempo even more. The move that helped was to play quiet music – the children settled to listen and it appeared to soothe them. The new quietness gave her a chance to speak more softly and she was able to establish a gentler atmosphere in her classroom. Unfortunately some of the children volunteered to bring in some of their music. Pop music immediately raised the tempo again and had to be banned to Friday afternoons.

Example 2 Using rhythm

Moira tells of her experience with twins with autism.

> It was extremely hard to persuade the boys to come into the nursery at all and some days they just sat by the door. They seemed aware that there were two of them, but apart from some noises, there was no other apparent move to communicate. The bigger twin occasionally would come near the water tray and he would stay a little time if he was allowed to throw the water around. One day he had got really wet and he was allowing me to change his T-shirt when he relaxed against me. I realised I was stroking his back and he was being comforted by the action. When I got the action right, and that seemed

to be slowly and smoothly stroking his head and the back of his shoulders, he would hum 'mmmmm', and that was the only real communication we had. The stroking must have reduced his tactile sensitivity and eased him – I need more advice on other things to try. I don't think it should be a case of having to find out everything for myself.

NB Moira already had permission from the twins' parents to change the boys clothes if they got wet playing in the water, but suddenly she realised that stroking them could be interpreted as another kind of touching. As she was anxious to allay any fears that the parents could have and also to avert any charges of abuse, she spoke with them and demonstrated what she intended to do. The parents were grateful to have been consulted and glad to learn of another strategy that might be helpful in calming their children at home.

So, sometimes through trial and error and through trying strategies that have helped other children, ways to settle children or to stimulate them can be found. Sadly there is no recipe book to guarantee success every time, but when a breakthrough comes, no matter how small or how transient, it repays all the effort that goes into the planning and preparation and the repeated attempts to get it right.

When children are stressed they need to play; when they need to learn, they can play some more. Play activities can be structured so that the children learn at their own pace and enjoy the things that are important to them. Through these activities they can find success and through that gain confidence in attempting new things. Is this not what living and learning is all about? So if you ask children 'What did you do at school today?' and they reply 'We played', be thankful that they have been happily engrossed in doing many things. Be assured that they are learning too.

Play as progress and play as practice

Hutt (1979) differentiates between play as progress or learning and play as practice.

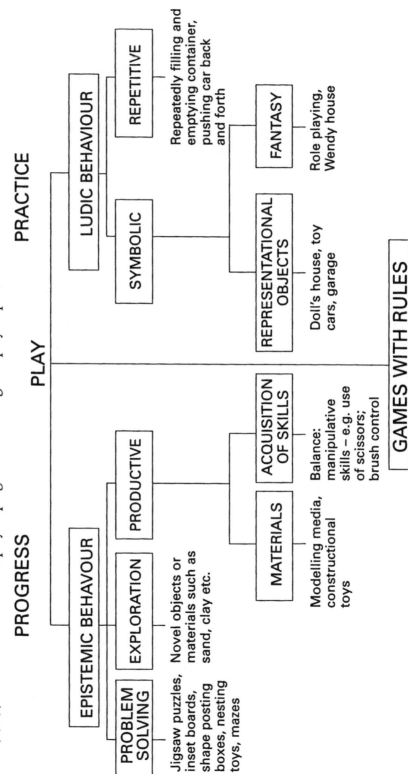

Play and learning: a selection of corners

Social Development

- Working cooperatively – setting a table, preparing meals for others
- Talking on the telephone, turn taking, being pleasant and helpful
- Acting out roles, recognising lead roles, subservient roles
- Tidying, being responsible
- Coping with disagreements and reaching a compromise

Perceptual–motor Development

- Preparing meals – setting places at the table carefully
- Dressing the doll, fitting small garments, doing up buttons
- Tidying up, balancing dishes,
- Dialling the telephone
- Making a meal
- Dressing up

Home Corner

Emotional Development

- Acting out different roles – appreciating the nuances of each, e.g. caring for baby, learning to pretend
- Preparing a matching table – choice of dishes, tablecloth, colour, shape. Appreciation of presentation and 'looking good'
- Selecting suitable clothes for doll either in terms of weather or fashion
- Making a meal – appreciating what is needed for each meal

Intellectual Development

- Talking on the telephone, making suggestions, imagining responses
- 1:1 correspondence (is there a plate for every doll?)
- Planning and making a meal – choosing ingredients for healthy eating
- Language, e.g. responding to suggestions, giving alternative ideas, listening to others, making suggestions, learning new words
- Solving problems with a partner or in a small group

Figure A2.1 Learning in the home corner

Social Development

- Cooperating with each other to compose a tune

- Listening and waiting for turns

- Sharing instruments

- Talking with friends and adults about the music

Perceptual–motor Development

- Coordination – two hands working together to play instruments

- Rhythmical training, keeping the beat

- Controlling length of sound

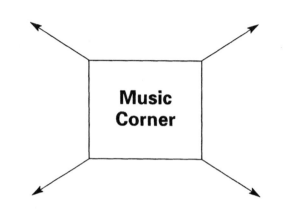

Music Corner

Emotional Development

- Investigating and appreciating different sounds

- Responding to sounds (movement, language)

- Understanding how sounds can represent ideas, e.g. fire crackling, rain pattering

- Selecting words to describe sounds

Intellectual Development

- Recognising sounds made by different instruments

- Counting the beat

- Learning the names of the instruments

- Learning words of songs

- Basic composition

- Planning what comes next

Figure A2.2 Learning in the music corner

Social Development

- Cooperating/discussing a patient's illness

- Development of altruism through caring for someone else

- Working together to discuss how to cope, what is to be done, how news is to go home

- Being responsible for someone else

Perceptual–motor Development

- Handling small equipment

- Rolling bandages

- Dialling the telephone

- Gently handling a sore arm/leg/head

- Placing a stethoscope or hypodermic

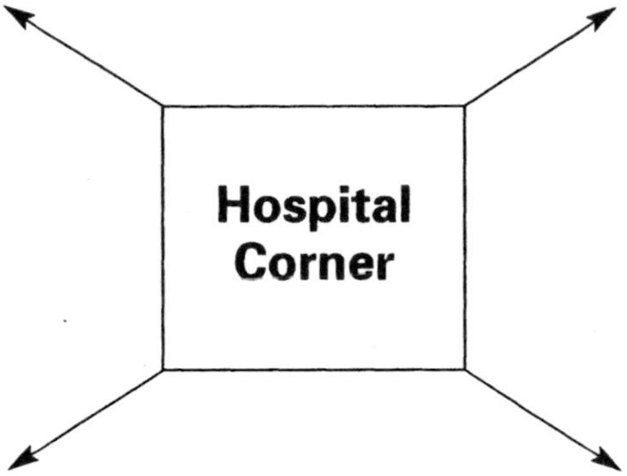

Hospital Corner

Emotional Development

- Role play – appreciation of different personnel

- Appreciating hospital procedures

- Respecting/understanding disability

- Confronting the idea of dying

Intellectual Development

- Learning about medicines

- Safety awareness

- S.O.S. awareness

- New 'hospital' vocabulary

Figure A2.3 Learning in the hospital corner

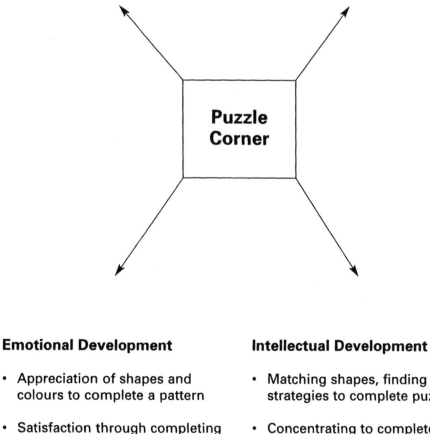

Social Development

- Taking turns

- Sharing puzzles

- Waiting

- Cooperating with a friend/in a small group

Perceptual–motor Development

- Fine motor skill development – lifting and placing puzzle pieces with pincer grip

- Throwing dice – judging strength, timing of release

- Crossing the midline to place pieces

Puzzle Corner

Emotional Development

- Appreciation of shapes and colours to complete a pattern

- Satisfaction through completing a puzzle

- Matching colours and designs

Intellectual Development

- Matching shapes, finding strategies to complete puzzle

- Concentrating to complete puzzle

- Language development, e.g. describing shapes and pictures

Figure A2.4 Learning in the puzzle corner

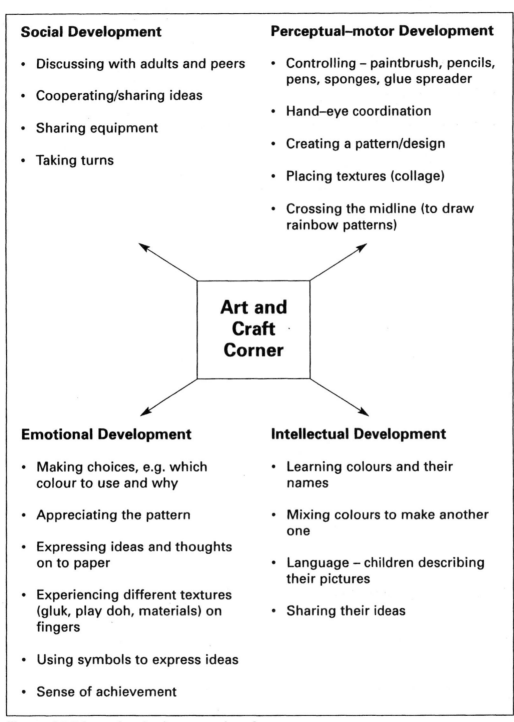

Social Development

- Discussing with adults and peers
- Cooperating/sharing ideas
- Sharing equipment
- Taking turns

Perceptual–motor Development

- Controlling – paintbrush, pencils, pens, sponges, glue spreader
- Hand–eye coordination
- Creating a pattern/design
- Placing textures (collage)
- Crossing the midline (to draw rainbow patterns)

Art and Craft Corner

Emotional Development

- Making choices, e.g. which colour to use and why
- Appreciating the pattern
- Expressing ideas and thoughts on to paper
- Experiencing different textures (gluk, play doh, materials) on fingers
- Using symbols to express ideas
- Sense of achievement

Intellectual Development

- Learning colours and their names
- Mixing colours to make another one
- Language – children describing their pictures
- Sharing their ideas

Figure A2.5 Learning in the art and craft corner

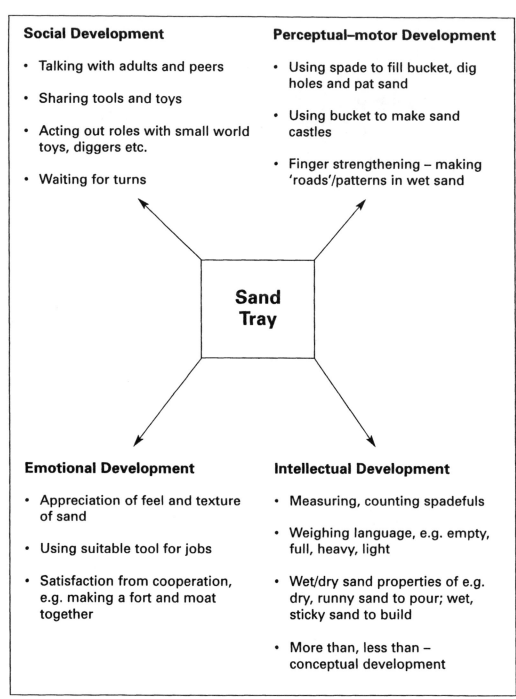

Social Development

- Talking with adults and peers

- Sharing tools and toys

- Acting out roles with small world toys, diggers etc.

- Waiting for turns

Perceptual–motor Development

- Using spade to fill bucket, dig holes and pat sand

- Using bucket to make sand castles

- Finger strengthening – making 'roads'/patterns in wet sand

Sand Tray

Emotional Development

- Appreciation of feel and texture of sand

- Using suitable tool for jobs

- Satisfaction from cooperation, e.g. making a fort and moat together

Intellectual Development

- Measuring, counting spadefuls

- Weighing language, e.g. empty, full, heavy, light

- Wet/dry sand properties of e.g. dry, runny sand to pour; wet, sticky sand to build

- More than, less than – conceptual development

Figure A2.6 Learning in the sand tray

Social Development

- Conveying ideas to one another

- Cooperating to carry out plan

- Being prepared to take role, e.g. bus driver or passenger

Perceptual–motor Development

- Handling chosen materials

- Gluing/painting

- Supporting boxes to make fantasy items

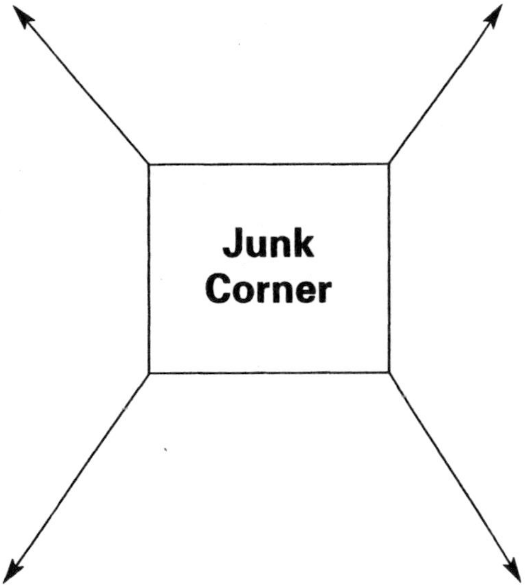

Junk Corner

Emotional Development

- Appreciating the possible outcome

- Weighing up different possibilities and choosing

- Pretending, e.g. that the spaceship has taken off

Intellectual Development

- Conceptualising ideas

- Making decisions

- Planning the stages of putting the object together

Figure A2.7 Learning in the junk corner

Social Development

- Waiting, taking turns

- Cooperating, e.g. on see-saw

- Working with/avoiding others

Perceptual–motor Development

- Running, climbing, balancing – all gross motor skills

- Throwing and catching, kicking – all ball skills

- Crawling up and down, on and off

Outdoor Play on Large Aparatus

Emotional Development

- Contributing to self-esteem

- Confidence in meeting new challenges

- Release of stress, e.g. in running freely

Intellectual Development

- Learning to balance

- Judging how much strength/ speed/momentum is needed

- Planning the sequence of movement

Figure A2.8 Learning to move on large apparatus

Early learning goals (QCA 2001)

The early learning goals, set by the Qualifications and Curriculum Authority, are goals which it is hoped children will achieve by the end of the primary school reception year when most are nearly six.

Areas of learning and early learning goals

The foundation stage is organised in six areas of learning:

- personal, social and emotional development
- language and literacy
- mathematical development
- knowledge and understanding of the world
- physical development
- creative development

Early learning goals for personal, social and emotional development

By the end of the foundation stage, most children will:

- continue to be interested, excited and motivated to learn;
- be confident to try new activities, initiate ideas and speak in a familiar group;
- maintain attention, concentrate, and sit quietly when appropriate;
- have a developing awareness of their own needs, views and feelings and be sensitive to the needs, views and feelings of others;
- have a developing respect for their own cultures and beliefs and those of other people;
- respond to significant experiences, showing a range of feelings when appropriate;
- form good relationships with adults and peers;

- work as part of a group or class, taking turns and sharing fairly, understanding that there need to be agreed values and codes of behaviour for groups of people, including adults and children, to work together harmoniously;
- understand what is right, what is wrong, and why;
- dress and undress independently and manage their own personal hygiene;
- select and use activities and resources independently;
- consider the consequences of their words and actions for themselves and others;
- understand that people have different needs, views, cultures and beliefs, which need to be treated with respect;
- understand that they can expect others to treat their needs, views, cultures and beliefs with respect.

Early learning goals for language and literacy

- enjoy listening to and using spoken and written language, and readily turn to it in their play and learning;
- explore and experiment with sounds, words and texts;
- listen with enjoyment and respond to stories, songs and other music, rhymes and poems and make their own stories, songs, rhymes and poems;
- use language to imagine and recreate roles and experiences;
- use talk to organise, sequence and clarify thinking, ideas, feelings and events;
- sustain attentive listening, responding to what they have heard by relevant comments, questions or actions;
- interact with others, negotiating plans and activities and taking turns in conversation;
- extend their vocabulary, exploring the meanings and sounds of new words;
- retell narratives in the correct sequence, drawing on the language patterns of stories;
- speak clearly and audibly with confidence and control and show awareness of the listener, for example by their use of conventions such as greetings, 'please' and 'thank you';
- hear and say initial and final sounds in words, and short vowel sounds within words;
- link sounds to letters, naming and sounding the letters of the alphabet;
- read a range of familiar and common words and simple sentences independently;
- know that print carries meaning and, in English, is read from left to right and top to bottom;
- show understanding of elements of stories, such as main character, sequence of events, and openings, and how information can be found in non-fiction texts to answer questions about where, who, why and how;

- attempt writing for various purposes, using features of different forms, such as lists, stories, instructions;
- write their own names and other things such as labels and captions and begin to form simple sentences, sometimes using punctuation;
- use their phonic knowledge to write simple regular words and make phonetically plausible attempts at more complex words;
- use a pencil and hold it effectively to form recognisable letters, most of which are correctly formed.

Early learning goals for mathematical development

- say and use number names in order in familiar contexts;
- count reliably up to ten everyday objects;
- recognise numerals 1 to 9;
- use language such as 'more' or 'less', 'greater' or 'smaller', 'heavier' or 'lighter', to compare two numbers or quantities;
- in practical activities and discussion begin to use the vocabulary involved in adding and subtracting;
- find one more or one less than a number from 1 to 10;
- begin to relate addition to combining two groups of objects, and subtraction to 'taking away';
- talk about, recognise and recreate simple patterns;
- use language such as 'circle' or 'bigger' to describe the shape and size of solids and flat shapes;
- use everyday words to describe position;
- use developing mathematical ideas and methods to solve practical problems.

Early learning goals for knowledge and understanding of the world

- investigate objects and materials by using all of their senses as appropriate;
- find out about, and identify some features of, living things, objects and events they observe;
- look closely at similarities, differences, patterns and change;
- ask questions about why things happen and how things work;
- build and construct with a wide range of objects, selecting appropriate resources, and adapting their work where necessary;
- select the tools and techniques they need to shape, assemble and join the materials they are using;
- find out about and identify the uses of everyday technology and use ICT and programmable toys to support their learning;

- find out about past and present events in their own lives, and in those of their families and other people they know;
- observe, find out about, and identify features in the place they live and the natural world;
- begin to know about their own cultures and beliefs and those of other people;
- find out about their environment, and talk about those features they like and dislike.

Early learning goals for physical development

- move with confidence, imagination and in safety;
- move with control and coordination;
- show awareness of space, of themselves and of others;
- recognise the importance of keeping healthy and those things which contribute to this;
- recognise the changes that happen to their bodies when they are active;
- use a range of small and large equipment;
- travel around, under, over and through balancing and climbing equipment;
- handle tools, objects, construction and malleable materials safely and with increasing control.

Early learning goals for creative development

- explore colour, texture, shape, form and space in two and three dimensions;
- recognise and explore how sounds can be changed, sing simple songs from memory, recognise repeated sounds and sound patterns and match movements to music;
- respond in a variety of ways to what they see, hear, smell, touch and feel;
- use their imagination in art and design, music, dance, imaginative and role play, and stories;
- express and communicate their ideas, thoughts and feelings by using a widening range of materials, suitable tools, imaginative and role play, movement, designing and making, and a variety of songs and musical instruments.

A developmental record

Child's name:_____

Age: _____(years)_____(months)   Sex: Male ☐   Female ☐

Place in family: ☐   ☐   ☐   ☐
                   1st   2nd   3rd   4th child

This checklist is for one child who is causing concern. Please record the child's usual level of competency against each criterion. If erratic behaviour makes this difficult, please say so.

Please tick where appropriate and add any other area of concern or provide details that would illuminate any assessment. Thank you for doing this.

First some general observations:

Does the child have	Yes	No	Details
(a) poor sight?	☐	☐	
(b) poor hearing?	☐	☐	
(c) a physical disability?	☐	☐	
(d) difficulty understanding instructions?	☐	☐	
(e) speech difficulties?	☐	☐	
(i) articulation	☐	☐	
(ii) poor vocabulary	☐	☐	
(f) body build problems?	☐	☐	
(i) overweight	☐	☐	
(ii) fragile	☐	☐	
(iii) low muscle tone	☐	☐	
(iv) a recent worrying change	☐	☐	
(g) any allergies?	☐	☐	
(h) any regular medication?	☐	☐	
(i) a history of birth difficulties? e.g.	☐	☐	
(i) prematurity	☐	☐	
(ii) oxygen deprivation	☐	☐	

Is the child   Yes   No   Details

(j) very tense and unsure?   ☐   ☐
(k) aggressive?   ☐   ☐
(l) prone to behavioural swings? ☐   ☐
(m) lethargic?   ☐   ☐
(n) lacking concentration?   ☐   ☐
(o) attention seeking?   ☐   ☐
(p) over active?   ☐   ☐

Has there been any significant recent change?

If so, please explain.

The checklist now asks you to tick one box for each competence then give a mark out of ten for 'general coping ability' in that field. The boxes are generally: 'yes, can do it'; 'some difficulty' (meaning that the child needs real effort to cope); 'severe difficulty' (meaning that the child does not cope) and 'regression' (meaning that the child's performance is getting worse). Please say if any illness has caused a temporary regression, which you would expect to be overcome quickly, or if the difficulties have lasted for a long time, note that too. Any information is very helpful.

Intellectual skills

Can the child		Yes, can do it	Some diffi- culty	Severe diffi- culty	Regression	Please give details
(a)	talk readily to adults?					
(b)	talk readily to children?					
(c)	use a wide vocabulary?					
(d)	use contextually appropriate vocabulary?					
(e)	recall recent events readily?					
(f)	follow a sequence of (three) instructions?					
(g)	engage in pretend play?					
(h)	understand: spatial concepts – under, over, through?					
	mathematical concepts – bigger, smaller?					
(i)	organise themselves/ plan what to do next?					

Give the child a mark out of ten for general intellectual competence. ☐

Please add details below if appropriate.

Social skills

Can the child		Yes, can do it	Some diffi- culty	Severe diffi- culty	Regression	Please give details
(a)	interact easily with adults?					
(b)	interact easily with children?					
(c)	converse readily?					
(d)	take turns with no fuss?					
(e)	take the lead in some activities?					
(f)	participate in someone else's game?					
(g)	make a friend?					
(h)	keep a friend?					
(i)	understand how others feel?					
(j)	shrug off unwanted comments?					
(k)	approach new experiences confidently?					
(l)	join in games willingly?					

Give a mark out of ten for general social competence. ☐

Please add details below if appropriate.

Emotional skills

	Does the child	Never	Some-times	Usually	Regression	Please give details
(a)	cling to a carer?					
(b)	appear aloof, withdrawn?					
(c)	keep eye contact?					
(d)	understand personal space?					
(e)	show tactile oversensitivity?					
(f)	appear defiant/ stubborn?					
(g)	disturb others?					
(h)	move constantly (i.e. is hyperactive)?					
(i)	have outbursts of rage?					
(j)	appear docile but 'lost'?					

Give a mark out of ten for general emotional competence. ☐

Please add details below if appropriate.

Gross motor skills

Can the child	Yes, can do it	Some diffi-culty	Severe diffi-culty	Regression	Please give details
(a) stand still, balanced and in control?					
(b) sit still without slumping?					
(c) walk smoothly with a good sense of poise?					
(d) turn corners efficiently?					
(e) walk on tiptoe (count of six)?					
(f) jump (two feet off floor)?					
(g) crawl?					
(h) kick a stationary ball?					
(i) catch and throw a ball when passed sympathetically?					
(j) roll sideways (pencil) and come back to standing easily?					

Give a mark out of ten for general gross motor competence. ☐

Please add details below if appropriate.

Fine motor skills

Can the child	Yes, can do it	Some diffi- culty	Severe diffi- culty	Regression	Please give details
(a) use a pencil with control?					
(b) spread toast?					
(c) pass a ball from one hand to the other easily?					
(d) fasten buttons?					
(e) draw a rainbow without changing hands?					
(f) pick up a small object, e.g a bead easily?					
(g) replace it carefully (letting go at the right time)?					
(h) chew food with mouth closed?					
(i) suck through a straw?					

Give a mark out of ten for general fine motor competence. ☐

Please add details below if appropriate.

Please say:

Is the child's behaviour erratic: ☐   ☐

                                      Yes   No

Thank you for completing this.

Places to get help

ADHD

The Secretary
Hyperactive Children's Support Group
71 Whyke Lane
Chichester
West Sussex PO19 2LD

Asperger's syndrome

National Autistic Society (Scotland)
Central Chambers
109 Hope Street
Glasgow G2 6LL
Email: scotland@nas.org.uk
www.nas.org.uk

I CAN
4 Dyer's Building
Holborn
London EC1N 2QP
Tel: 0870 010 4066

The National Autistic Society
393 City Road
Stratford
London EC1V 1NG
Tel: 020 7833 2299
Helpline: 0870 600 8585

Autism/autistic disorder/childhood autism/infantile autism

The Scottish Society for Autism
Hilton House
Alloa Business Park
Whins Road
Alloa FK10 3SA
Tel: 01259 720044
Fax: 01259 720051
www.autism-in-scotland.org.uk/main.html

National Autistic Society (Scotland)
Central Chambers
109 Hope Street
Glasgow G2 6LL
Tel: 0141 221 8090
Fax: 0141 221 8118
Email: scotland@nas.org.uk
www.nas.org.uk

SCA (Scottish Centre for Autism)
(Consultant psychiatrist: Dr John Shemilt)
Department of Child and Family Psychiatry
Royal Hospital for Sick Children
Glasgow G3 8SJ
Tel: 0141 201 0000

Bullying

CURB (Children Under Risk from
  Bullying)
Maureen Booth-Martin
Heath
Cardiff CF4 3NT
Tel: 029 2061 1300

Cluttering

Royal College of Speech and Language
  Therapists
(RCSLT)
2 White Hart Yard
London SE1 1NX
Tel: 020 7378 1200

Department of Speech and Language
  Sciences
Queen Margaret University College
Clerwood Terrace
Edinburgh EH12 8TS
Tel: 0131 317 3682
Fax: 0131 317 3689
www.sls.qmuc.ac.uk

Developmental language delay/disorder

Royal College of Speech and Language
  Therapists
(RCSLT)
2 White Hart Yard
London SE1 1NX
Tel: 020 7378 1200

Kim Hartley (Scottish coordinator for
  the RCSLT)
34/4 Kirk Street
Edinburgh EH6 5EZ
Tel/Fax: 0131 476 2666
Email: kim.hartley@rcslt.org.uk

Down's syndrome

Down's Syndrome Association
153–155 Mitcham Road
London SW17 9PG
Tel: 020 8682 4001
Email: info@downs-syndrome.org.uk
www.downs-syndrome.org.uk/

Scottish Down's Syndrome Association
158/160 Balgreen Road
Edinburgh EH11 3AU
Tel: 0131 313 4225
Fax: 0131 313 4285
Email: info@sdsa.org.uk
www.sdsa.org.uk

Dyslexia/specific learning difficulties

British Dyslexia Foundation
98 London Road
Reading
Berkshire
Tel: 01734 662677

The Scottish Dyslexia Association
Stirling Business Centre
Wellgreen
Stirling FK8 2DZ
Tel: 01786 446650
Fax: 01786 471235

Dyslexia Scotwest (The Dyslexia
    Institute)
74 Victoria Crescent Road
Dowanhill
Glasgow G12 9JN
Tel: 0141 334 4549
Fax: 0141 339 8879

The Dyslexia Research Trust
Magdalen College
Oxford OX1 4AU
Tel: 0118 934 0580
Email: info@dyslexic.org.uk

Dyspraxia/apraxia

Dyspraxia Foundation
8 West Alley
Hitchin
Hertfordshire SG5 1EG
Tel: 01462 455016

Healthcall Discovery Centre
12 Cathedral Road
Cardiff CF9 1LJ
Tel: 029 2022 2011

The Nuffield Centre Dyspraxia
    Programme
Nuffield Hearing and Speech Centre
RNTNE Division of Royal Free
Hampstead NHS Trust
Grays Inn Road
London WC1X 8DA
Tel: 020 7915 1535

Video: 'Perceptual–motor programmes
for early years children (age 5, 6, 7)',
available from
MALTS
Edinburgh University
Holyrood Road
Edinburgh
EH8 8AQ

Inclusion

Parents for Inclusion
Unit 20
70 South Lambeth Road
London SW8 1RL
Tel: 020 7735 7735

Selective mutism

SMIRA (Selective Mutism Information
    and Research Association)
13 Humberstone Drive
Leicester LE5 0RE
Tel: 0116 212 7411

Semantic and pragmatic disorders

Department of Educational Support
    and Guidance
Faculty of Education
University of Strathclyde
Jordanhill Campus
Glasgow G13 1PP
Tel: 0141 950 3330
Fax: 0141 950 3129
Email: edsupport@strath.ac.uk

SCA (Scottish Centre for Autism)
(Consultant psychiatrist: Dr John
    Shemilt)
Department of Child and Family
    Psychiatry
Royal Hospital for Sick Children
Glasgow G3 8SJ
Tel: 0141 201 0000

Department of Speech and Language
    Sciences
Queen Margaret University College
Clerwood Terrace
Edinburgh EH12 8TS
Tel: 0131 317 3682
Fax: 0131 317 3689
www.sls.qmuc.ac.uk

Specific language impairment

Dockrell, J. and Messer, D. (1999)
    *Children's Language and Communication
    Difficulties.* London: Cassell.
Donaldson, M. L. (1995) *Children with
    Language Impairments.* London: Jessica
    Kingsley.

I CAN
4 Dyer's Buildings
Holburn
London EC1N 2QP
Tel: 0870 010 4066

Royal College of Speech and Language
    Therapists
(RCSLT)
2 White Hart Yard
London SE1 1NX
Tel: 020 7378 1200

Speech and language difficulties

Afasic
50–52 Great Sutton Street
London EC1V 0DJ
Tel: 020 7490 9410
Fax: 020 7251 2834
Helpline: 0845 355 5577 (local call
rate)
Email: info@afasic.org.uk
www.afasic.org.uk

Afasic Scotland
93 Dunoon Terrace
Dundee DD2 2DG
Tel: 01382 666 560
Fax: 01382 641 177
Email: afasicscot@aol.com

Bibliography

Afasic (Scotland) (2000) *Glossary Sheets*. Dundee: Scottish Executive.

Alton, S. (1998) 'Differentiation not discrimination: Delivering the curriculum for Down's syndrome in mainstream schools', *Support for Learning* 13(4).

Arcelus, J. and Munden, A. C. (1999) *Symptoms of ADHD and Emotional and Behavioural Disturbance in Children from Mainstream Education*. London: Jessica Kingsley Publications.

Atkins, J. and Bastiani, J. (1988) *Listening to Parents: An approach to the improvement of home–school relations*. London: Croom Helm.

Attwood, T. (1998) *Asperger's Syndrome: A guide for parents and professionals*. London: Jessica Kinsley Publishers.

Ayres, J. A. (1972) *Sensory Integration and Learning Disorders*. Los Angeles: Western Psychological Services.

British Dyslexia Association (1999) *Fact Sheet*. Reading: The British Dyslexia Association.

Bruner, J. (1966) *The Process of Education*. Cambridge, MA: Harvard University Press.

Burgoine, E. and Wing, L. (1983) 'Identical triplets with Asperger's syndrome', *British Journal of Psychiatry* 33, 1169–1182.

Caan, W. (1998) 'Foreword', in Portwood, M. (ed.) *Developmental Dyspraxia, Identification and Intervention: A manual for parents and professionals*, 2nd edn. London: David Fulton Publishers.

Campbell, S. B. and Pierce, E. W. (1991) 'Non-compliant behaviour, overactivity and family stress and negative maternal control with preschool children', *Development and Psychopathology* 3.

Chazan, M. *et al.* (1987) *Teaching Five to Eight Year Olds*. London: Blackwell.

Chasty, J. S. (1990) 'Meeting the challenge of specific learning difficulties', in Pumfrey, P. and Elliot, C. (eds) *Reading, Writing and Spelling*. London: Falmer Press.

Chesson, R. *et al.* (1990) *The Child with Motor/Learning Difficulties*. Aberdeen: Royal Aberdeen Children's Hospital.

Clough, P. and Corbett, J. (2000) *Theories of Inclusive Education*. London: Paul Chapman Publishing.

Cooley, C. (1962) *Human Nature and the Social Order*. New York: Charles Scribner.

Croll, P. and Moses, D. (1995) *One in Five*. London: Routledge and Kegan Paul.

Department for Education and Employment (2000) *Curriculum Guidance for the Foundation Stage*. London: QCA.

Dighe, A. and Kettles, G. (1996) 'Developmental dyspraxia: an overview', in Reid, G. (ed.) *Dimensions of Dyslexia, Vol 2 Literacy, Language and Learning*. Edinburgh: Moray House Institute of Education.

Dyspraxia Foundation (1999) *Praxis Makes Perfect 2*. Hitchin: The Dyspraxia Foundation.

East Lothian Council (2000) *Anti-bullying: Guidelines and procedures for young people*. Haddington: Dept of Education and Community Services.

Ehlers, S. and Gillberg, C. (1993) 'The epidemiology of Asperger's syndrome – a total population study', *Journal of Child Psychology and Psychiatry* 34.

Eron, L. D. *et al.* (1991) 'The role of parental variables in the learning of aggression', in Peplre, D. J. (ed.) *The Development and Treatment of Childhood Aggression*. Hillside, NJ: Erlbaum.

Farnham-Diggory, S. (1992) *The Learning Disabled Child*. Cambridge, MA: Harvard University Press.

Goddard, S. (1996) *A Teacher's Window into the Child's Mind*. Eugene, Oregon: Fern Ridge Press.

Gurney, P. (1987) 'Self-esteem enhancement in children: a review of research findings', *Educational Research* 29(2).

Hallidie-Smith, K. A. (1987) 'The heart', in Lane, D. and Stratford, B. (eds) *Current Approaches to Down's Syndrome*. Gillingham, Kent: Cassell.

Harter, S. (1990) 'Processes underlying adolescent self-concept formation', in Montemayor, R. *et al.* (eds) *From Childhood to Adolescence: A transitional period?* Newbury Park, CA: Sage Publications.

Healy, J. (1996) 'Why can't they pay attention? Attention deficit disorders and learning disabilities', in Reid, G. (ed.) *Dimensions of Dyslexia, Vol 2 Literacy, Language and Learning*. Edinburgh: Moray House Institute of Education.

Houston, M. *et al.* (1996) 'Phonemic awareness and concepts of print in the nursery school', in Reid, G. (ed.) *Dimensions of Dyslexia, Vol 2 Literacy, Language and Learning*. Edinburgh: Moray House Institute of Education.

Hutt, C. (1979) 'Exploration and play', in Sutton-Smith, B. (ed.) *Play and Learning*. London: Gardner Press.

Hutt, S. J. *et al.* (1987) *Play, Exploration and Learning*. London: Routledge.

Isaacs, S. (1933) *Social Development in Young Children*. London: Routledge.

Jordan, R. and Powell, S. (1996) *Understanding and Teaching Children with Autism*. Chichester: John Wiley.

Keen, D. (2001) 'Comorbidity of syndromes'. Paper presented at the Durham Conference on Dyspraxia. University of Durham.

Lally, M. (1991) *The Nursery Teacher in Action*. London: Paul Chapman.

Maccoby, E. E. (1990) *Social Development, Psychological Growth and the Parent–Child Relationship*. New York: Harcourt Brace Janovich.

McGuinness, D. (1985) *When Children Don't Learn.* New York: Basic Books.

Macintyre, C. (2000) *Dyspraxia in the Early Years.* London: David Fulton Publishers.

Macintyre, C. (2001) *Enhancing Learning through Play.* London: David Fulton Publishers.

Munden, A. and Arcelus, J. (1999) *The AD/HD Handbook.* London: Jessica Kingsley Publishers.

Munn, P. (1994) 'The early development of literacy and numeracy', *European Early Childhood Education Research Journal* 2(1).

Piaget, J. (1969) *The Psychology of the Child.* New York: Basic Books.

Piaget, J. (1977) *The Development of Thought: Equilibration of cognitive structures.* New York: Viking Press.

Pope, M. (1988) 'Dyspraxia: a head teacher's perspective', in *Praxis Makes Perfect.* Hitchin: The Dyspraxia Trust.

Qualifications and Curriculum Authority (2001) *Early Learning Goals.* London: QCA.

Reid, G. (ed.) (1996) *Dimensions of Dyslexia, Vol 2 Literacy, Language and Learning.* Edinburgh: Moray House Institute of Education.

Reilly, M. (1974) *Play as Exploratory Learning.* Beverly Hills, CA: Sage Publications.

Richardson, A. (2000) 'Dyslexia, dyspraxia and ADHD. Can nutrition help?' Paper presented at the Durham Conference on Dyspraxia: University of Durham.

Robinson, N. (1996) 'Role of the speech therapist', in Reid, G. (ed.) *Dimensions of Dyslexia, Vol 2 Literacy, Language and Learning.* Edinburgh: Moray House Institute of Education.

Rubin, K. H. *et al.* (1983) 'Play', in Hetherington, E. M. (ed.) *Handbook of Child Psychology: Socialization, personality and social development,* Vol.4. New York: Wiley.

Scottish Consultative Committee on the Curriculum (1999) *Promoting Learning: Assessing children's progress 3–5.* Dundee: SOEID.

Sonken, P. and Stiff, B. (1991) *Show Me What My Friends Can See.* London: Wolfsen Centre Institute of Child Health, Great Ormond St Hospital.

Stein, J. (2000) 'Stepping forward'. Paper presented at the Durham Conference on Dyspraxia. University of Durham.

Thomson, S. K. (1975) 'Gender labels and early sex-role development', *Child Development* 46.

Tredwell, S. J. *et al.* (1990) 'Instability of the upper cervical spine in Down's Syndrome', *Journal of Pediatric Orthopedics* 10(5).

Trevarthen, C. (1993) *Play for Tomorrow.* Edinburgh: Edinburgh University Video Production.

Vygotsky, L. S. (1978) *Mind and Society.* Cambridge, MA: Harvard University Press.

Wood, L. and Bennett, N. (1997) 'The rhetoric and reality of play: teachers' thinking and classroom practice', in *Early Years, The Professional Association of Early Years Education* 2.

Index